CYBER SHOCK

Cyberattacks that shook the World

AJAY SINGH

ATLANTIC
PUBLISHERS & DISTRIBUTORS (P) LTD

7/22, Ansari Road, Darya Ganj, New Delhi
Tel.: +91-11-4077 5252, 2327 3880
E-mail: orders@atlanticbooks.com
Web: www.atlanticbooks.com

Published by Atlantic Publishers & Distributors (P) Ltd 2024

Printed & bound in India by Atlantic Print Services

To My Parents

Late Mr Pratap Singh, IPS (Retd.),
and my mother,
Mrs Indira Pratap Singh,
who planted the seed of knowledge
in my mind and
nurtured it.

Cyber Shock

"A state of disbelief, anxiety and panic that arises from receiving the news or discovering that you (individual or organisation) have been the target/victim of a cyberattack, data breach or online scam".

– Ajay Singh

Acknowledgements

Creating a book is always a challenging endeavour, no matter how many times you have done it before. It is difficult because readability matters, because details matter, and authenticity matters, and there are often many details to consider.

I would like to express my sincere gratitude to Atlantic Publishers and Distributors, for publishing, and distributing this book.

My heartfelt appreciation to the editorial team–Dr Manisha Mathews and Namarita for their diligent work in editing and publication of this book.

I would also like to acknowledge the support, encouragement, and patience of my family while I was occupied with devoting my time and attention to writing this book.

Contents

Introduction

Cybercrimes have evolved rapidly, growing in frequency, scale and sophistication over the years. Cybercriminals have now become organised, well-resourced and have different motivations. Cyberattacks are the bread and butter for cybercriminals, and cyberspace is their warzone. According to Security Magazine, there are over 2,200 cyberattacks each day, which translates to one cyberattack every 39 seconds (Fox, 2022).

As they say, war is a constant, and this is true even for the digital world, where war (cyberattacks) happens frequently. War for power, money, supremacy and even leverage. This war is fought at various levels and in different ways, but cyberattacks are the primary means. Cyberattacks bring into play a wide array of cyber techniques and weapons, where deceit is cloaked in technology, where things move rapidly without any warning, where adversaries are unknown, and the destruction and damage are disproportionate to the costs incurred by the attackers. All in all, this is warfare of a different kind. Deadly, disruptive and potentially devastating. Pundits predict that the '9/11 moment' of cyberattacks is yet to come. Some go on to say that it will come sooner than later.

A cyberattack is any attempt by cybercriminals using computers and related technologies to gain unauthorised entry into computer systems or digital networks. It is done with the intent to maliciously disable computers, disrupt organisations, bring businesses to a standstill, steal data or use a breached computer as an entry point for other attacks. The fallout of successful cyberattacks is often a trail of financial losses and damaged reputations.

Cyberattacks arouse a sense of curiosity and interest among us as we want to understand more about what is happening. The scale of damage, deception, sophistication and motives are all common ingredients of major cyberattacks, while the use of technology and tactics constitute the operating elements. In the aftermath of a cyberattack, victims have to deal with the ensuing crisis, loss, chaos and the overwhelming sense of being violated. Furthermore, major cyberattacks receive immense media attention, and those responsible for security are often scrutinised for their actions. This makes the task of incident handling more challenging as it requires undertaking recovery tasks even while attending to media queries.

The famous SolarWinds cyberattack is a case in point. Ever since its discovery, the 'SolarWinds hack' has been receiving media attention worldwide. It is being touted as one of the biggest ever cyberattacks targeted against the US government, its agencies, and several other private companies. In fact, it is more than likely that it is not just limited to the US but a global cyberattack. The potential implications of the attack and the novel tactics employed by the attackers have grabbed world headlines. It shook large corporations and governments around the world and highlighted new security vulnerabilities in the cyber world. While experts busied themselves in deciphering the tactics used by the hackers and analysing various other aspects of the cyberattack, organisations and governments were trying to understand the possible impact of such attacks on their digital systems.

Even before the SolarWinds hack, there have been several deadly cyberattacks that have rocked the digital world. Each one represents the lurking dangers that may manifest themselves and accost us at some point as we become increasingly dependent on digital technologies and navigate the cyber world. This is neither the first deadly cyberattack that the world has seen nor, by any stretch of imagination, is it going to be the last.

As common digital citizens, we often think that matters related to cyberattacks are too complex to digest, and technology related aspects with their associated jargon may be beyond our comprehension. And yet, there is this great need for us to satisfy our curiosity about these deadly cyberattacks. We must also recognise that there are many issues beyond technology in these attacks, and each attack has a context and motive behind it that must be deciphered and understood to truly evaluate what actually happened.

Existence in the digital world is fraught with cyber risks that lurk beneath the surface. Only experts usually have the requisite technical skills, but to hack into a system, one also needs to learn and understand how people think and act. Hackers not only develop the acumen to bypass security controls but also become masters of the art of deception. With our growing digital existence, it is imperative that we develop an awareness and enhance our knowledge base to withstand the various types of cyber threats and challenges.

History can teach us many things which can equip us to meet future challenges. This book is for all those who want to explore, understand and learn from the deadly cyberattacks and cyber scams that shook the world. The best way to delve into the subject is to dissect various aspects of major cyberattacks that the world has faced. This not only helps to satisfy our curiosity and analyse the elements with their associated effects but also prepares us for the future. The need to learn more about cyberattacks and related security measures might be of use in the following ways (cisoportal.com, 2021):

- Avoid cyberattacks and be aware of cyber scams
- Reduce risks and minimise losses and damage
- Share related knowledge with friends, family and colleagues
- Keep our data safe
- Learn from mistakes made by others
- Be forewarned and forearmed

None of us like shocks and unpleasant surprises, whether at an individual level or an organisation level. For an individual, a cyber threat or becoming a victim of a cyber scam can be devastating and mentally disturbing. For an organisation, cyberattacks are random and unpredictable events that have the potential to cause adverse impacts on the operations and reputation of an enterprise. They can threaten its very existence if the attack is targeted at its critical systems.

The total cost of cybercrime is estimated to exceed USD 8 trillion by the end of 2023. This includes monetary losses, post-incident investments in security tools as well as services and expenditure on ancillary activities such as remediation, legal fees, fines, penalties and more. To deal with this cyber onslaught, organisations will spend more than USD 188.3 billion in 2023 alone (Morgan, 2022).

Learning from the world's deadliest cyberattacks and scams can help us anticipate future threats, minimise losses and direct cybersecurity investments for maximum effectiveness.

The term 'anatomy' is often associated with biological sciences and living things, but in a broader sense, it refers to the structure or the internal working of any system. This book aims to study the anatomy of deadly cyberattacks that shook the world, to help us determine the motives, tactics, techniques, procedures deployed, the fallout, and most importantly glean the lessons we can learn from it.

The contents of this book are organised into twelve chapters.

Chapter One– ***Cyberattacks: Scourge of the 21st Century*** shows how cyberattacks are a top concern given the rise in their frequency and severity. It highlights how cyberattacks can be disruptive, destructive, devastating and even catastrophic through examples.

Chapter Two– ***Dynamics of a Cyberattack*** breaks down the elements of a cyberattack. It focuses on how threat actors develop their strategy and tactics based on their motives and how they use various techniques and deception to exploit security weaknesses to launch a variety of cyberattacks.

Chapter Three– ***Types of Cyberattacks: The Hackers' Dirty Dozen*** shows that there are numerous ways in which cyberattacks can be mounted. It encapsulates twelve key attack vectors that are deployed by hackers to launch cyberattacks, along with famous examples of such attacks.

Chapter Four– ***Another One Bites The Dust: The World's Biggest Data Breaches*** describes major data breaches that affected millions of people and became a source of financial and reputational losses for large corporations who were the custodians of their personal and sensitive data.

Chapter Five– ***Most Bizarre Cyberattacks*** dwells on those attacks that are out of the ordinary, unusual, or even weird where hackers have used tactics that could even be considered inconceivable.

Chapter Six– ***Held to Ransom: Major Extortion Attacks*** details major cyberattacks that paralysed or diminished the ability of companies to run normal operations in the face of ransomware attacks. These attacks not only severely impaired victim companies in carrying out their operations but impacted their customers as well.

Chapter Seven– ***Sneaking Through: Prominent Supply Chain Attacks*** is centred around cyber attacks launched via the supply chain also known as value-chain or third-party attacks. These occur when an attacker infiltrates a target system through an outside partner or provider with access to the organisation's systems and data. This chapter illustrates how hackers are increasingly using security weaknesses across the supply chain, including cloud systems, application programming interfaces and third-party system components.

Chapter Eight– ***The World's Biggest Cyberheists*** offers a ringside view of some major 'cyber heists', which, simply put, are robberies that take place on the internet. This chapter highlights instances like the Bangladesh Bank cyber heist, where hackers attempted to illegally transfer nearly USD 1 billion from the Federal Reserve Bank of New York account belonging to the Central Bank of Bangladesh.

Chapter Nine– ***Outsmarted: Top IoT Attacks*** shows how in the era of "smart-everything", hackers have a bigger playfield which is expanding rapidly. Experts say that everything being connected to the internet leaves us more vulnerable in-several ways. This chapter analyses how the proliferation of smart devices in our personal spaces and workspaces has led to major cyberattacks and data breaches. Today, digital twins are used to build virtual counterparts for (parts of) smart grids, building systems and manufacturing systems to understand and evaluate their complex underlying structures and processes. These virtual objects are closely tied to their physical counterparts, from which they extract data and run alongside in near real-time. Hackers can manipulate them, cause undesirable consequences and even endanger human safety.

Chapter Ten– ***Swindler's Inc.: Top Scams, Cons and Dirty Tricks*** sheds light on deception being the key element of all cyber scams and cons and talks about the ever-growing hackers' bag of dirty tricks. It explains over 50 types of cyber scams designed to cause harm and analyses the elements that are an integral part of them.

Chapter Eleven– ***Future Shock*** explains that even as we are coming to grips with existing attack vectors, new emerging threats and modes of attack keep coming up. It throws light on cyberattacks of the future and the resultant damage they can cause.

Chapter Twelve– ***Essential Cybersecurity Strategies for the Future*** is devoted to describing key strategies that can help minimise the impact of cyberattacks. Over 2,500 years ago, Sun Tzu, the Chinese military general, strategist, philosopher and writer, said in his book The Art of War, "In war, prepare for peace; in peace, prepare for war". In the cyber world, too, this dictum must be followed by organisations to minimise risks and be able to effectively deal with the cyber shocks of the future.

This book is based on three years of research, which involved going through many reports of cyberattacks. While I have made every attempt to ensure that there is no misrepresentation of events and related information, I cannot assume responsibility or any liability for the topicality, correctness, completeness, or quality of the information provided. My thanks to the readers who have picked up this book, and I hope that it will apprise them of the dangers lurking in the cyber world so that they can be better prepared to navigate their online activities safely and securely.

Ajay Singh

1

Cyberattacks: Scourge of the 21st Century

Cyberattacks have increasingly grown in scale, sophistication and the extent of damage they can cause. The frequency of such attacks is another key concern.

The World Economic Forum (WEF), in its Global Cybersecurity Outlook 2023 report, has warned that a "catastrophic cyber event" is likely in the next two years. In a survey, they found that 86 per cent of business leaders expected such an event, as did 93 per cent of cybersecurity leaders (World Economic Forum 2023a, 2023b). This may not come as a total surprise, given that we live in an environment supercharged by the threat of cyberattacks. These attacks are only increasing in frequency and severity, making cybercrime a big business that will become a $10.5 trillion industry by 2025, according to Cybersecurity Ventures (Morgan, 2020).

Professionalised cybercriminal groups today are more organised, have greater access to resources—technological as well as financial—and possess the ability to launch targeted cyberattacks using a wide array of tactics, techniques and procedures.

There is no single way to categorize cyberattacks. A simple way to categorize them is on the basis of motives of hackers, techniques used, or the harm caused by them. However, classifying them on their overall 'harm-quotient' is a useful way to understand the severity of their impact. Breaking them down further, we can label cyberattacks as disruptive, destructive, damaging, devastating or catastrophic, depending on the nature of the harm caused.

What does it take to classify a cyber incident as 'catastrophic'? Generally, cyberattacks that can cause the greatest amount of harm, with severe, widespread consequences, and are not limited to a specific industry or territory are considered part of this category. They can even be seen as the cyber-equivalent of a health pandemic.

While these are mere labels that help us categorise the impact or extent of harm caused, any cyberattack is a source of shock and potential loss for its victims. This is often because a cyberattack seemingly happens randomly, and everyone believes it will never happen to them. Even those who have previously experienced cyberattacks could prepare better to handle a future attack but they too believe that it will not happen to them again. Hence, whenever there is an instance of a cyberattack, no matter how limited or severe the consequences, there is always an element of shock. It would not be an overstatement to say that cyberattacks have become the scourge of the twenty-first century.

Colonial Pipeline Cyberattack (2021)

The Colonial Pipeline cyberattack of 2021 is a good example of a *disruptive* attack. The Colonial Pipeline is one of the longest and most important oil pipelines, transporting oil from the Gulf of Mexico to the East Coast of the US. The pipeline is 5,500 miles long and runs from Texas to New Jersey. It serves as a lifeline for gas consumers along the coastal states, including the airline industry, which requires jet fuel for many carriers, including American Airlines.

The attack started on the seventh of May as a ransomware attack and was initiated by attackers who entered the Colonial Pipeline network using an exposed password for a Virtual Private Network (VPN) account. This was possibly used by someone logging in to the corporate network from an outside location. From that point, the attack unfolded rapidly. The attackers stole one hundred gigabytes of data and infected the Colonial Pipeline IT network with ransomware that affected many vital systems, including billing and accounting.

Operations of the Colonial Pipeline were severely disrupted, and the management was forced to shut down the pipeline to prevent the ransomware from spreading. It was a well-planned multi-stage attack designed to disrupt operations and extort a ransom. Fortunately, the pipeline's operational technology systems that transport oil were not directly impacted during the attack. The news of the cyberattack led to panic-buying by consumers, resulting in shortages in many states. Instances of desperate consumers filling plastic bags with gasoline were also reported in some states (Mcfarland, 2021). There were long lines of consumers at gas stations as fuel supplies came to a complete halt. As the pipeline serves seventeen states that run along the Atlantic Coast from Maine to Florida. These states have a combined population of more than 120 million, which is almost 40 per cent of the country's total populace (Petrosyan, 2021). Soon, the attack was raised to the level of a national security threat, and even President Joe Biden had to declare a state of emergency.

A ransom demand was duly made by the attackers, and Colonial Pipeline paid them seventy-five Bitcoin (USD 4.4 million) to get the decryption key, enabling the company's Information Technology (IT) staff to regain control of its systems (Eaton & Volz, 2021). The pipeline restarted as normal operations resumed on May 12, 2021, within a week from when the cyberattack started.

Investigations by the Federal Bureau of Investigation (FBI) and other US security agencies were set in motion. The Colonial Pipeline hackers were reported to be a group known as DarkSide, thought to be operating out of Eastern Europe or Russia. The US Department of Justice's Ransomware and Digital Extortion Task Force recovered 63.7 bitcoin—approximately USD 2.3 million—a part of the total ransom paid to the attackers by following the money trail. The Colonial Pipeline ransomware attack is the largest publicly disclosed cyberattack against critical infrastructure in the US.

In the face of the disruption in the distribution of gas to its consumers, the Colonial Pipeline management team decided to pay the ransom in exchange for a decryption key that helped them recover access to their data and resume operations. Can payment of ransom be justified based on expediency? Most law enforcement agencies do not encourage, endorse, or condone the payment of ransom demands (NCSC, n.d.).

In the end, Colonial Pipeline got back a portion of the ransom paid, but in situations like these, there is no guarantee that an organisation will (a) get access to their data or computer systems, (b) will be able to fully disinfect computer systems, and (c) protect themselves from being targeted again.

Using a defense-in-depth strategy is a useful way of protecting an organisation against malware infections (NCSC, n.d.). Such a strategy is based on building layers of defense with several mitigations at each layer. This provides defenders more time and chances to detect malware and then allows them to stop it before it causes severe harm to the organisation.

Colonial Pipeline Ransomware Attack: A Timeline (Votiro, 2021)

6 May 2021	Hackers launch Colonial Pipeline cyberattack and steal 100 gigabytes of data before locking computers and demanding payment.
7 May 2021	Colonial Pipeline Company learns of the cyberattack. Informs law enforcement and other federal agencies. Engages cybersecurity experts. Temporarily halts all pipeline operations. Pays nearly USD 5 million to Eastern European hackers.
8 May 2021	The US Government assists in attack response.
9 May 2021	The Colonial Pipeline operations team develops a system restart plan.
11 May 2021	The company describes alternative fuel shipping strategies that are in place while they are making efforts to safely restore the pipeline.
12 May 2021	Colonial Pipeline restarts pipeline operations.
7 June 2021	Ransomware payment is partially recovered.

Aramco Cyberattack (2012)

Cyberattacks that are *destructive* make use of harmful malware such as wipers and modified ransomware to destroy data, eliminate traces of malicious activity or manipulate computer systems to render them inoperable. These kinds of attacks enable hackers to achieve strategic or tactical objectives involving the destruction of data and other IT devices. The attack on the Saudi Arabian oil giant Aramco is an example of one of the most destructive cyberattacks ever. In just a few hours, over 30,000 computers were wiped out or completely destroyed by the dreaded Shamoon virus (Pagliery, 2015).

Aramco is one of the most profitable and valuable companies in the world, owned by the Government of Saudi Arabia. The cyberattack began during the holy month of Ramadan when several employees were away from work. One of the computer technicians on Saudi Aramco's information technology team clicked on a dubious link which was part of a scam email, resulting in the attackers getting into Aramco's network.

The few employees who reported to work on the morning of August 15, 2012, were witness to flickering screens, disappearing files and computers shutting down on their own. The attack was on! The company soon went offline as offices around the world resorted to physically unplugging cables to prevent the virus from spreading.

The Shamoon virus (also known as W-32 DistTrack), which caused all the damage across 30,000 computers at Aramco, was discovered in 2012, targeting then-recent 32-bit NT kernel versions of Microsoft Windows. The virus gained notoriety for its destructive nature and the high costs of recovering from it. Shamoon can spread rapidly from an infected machine to other computers on the network. The virus works by compiling a list of files, uploading them to the attacker, and then erasing them. Further, it overwrites the Master Boot Record to make the computers unusable.

Suddenly, things had taken a dramatic turn for the worse, and Aramco's ability to supply 10 per cent of the world's oil was at risk. There was no internet at the office, and the corporate email was not operational. Office phones were also dead. A redeeming feature was that drilling and pumping operations, though automated, remained unaffected. However, this also posed a problem—the oil pumped out had to be supplied and invoiced to customers. Given that Aramco produced 9.5 million barrels of oil per day, the magnitude of this problem was immense.

All activities post-production had to be undertaken manually. The company was in crisis mode, and everything from managing supplies to contracting with governments and distribution partners was done using typewriters and fax machines. Meanwhile, Aramco had also suspended supplies through domestic gas tank trucks. After seventeen days, the corporation relented and started giving oil away for free to ensure availability within Saudi Arabia (Pagliery, 2015).

The responsibility for the cyberattack was claimed by a group that called itself the "Cutting Sword of Justice" as retribution for Aramco's support of the Al Saud royal family's authoritarian regime (CFR, 2012).

Once the initial shock of the cyberattack and its impact was temporarily taken care of by operating manually, the task of making the computer systems operational again had to be accomplished. This meant that more than 30,000 destroyed hard disk drives needed to be replaced. Aramco was determined to accomplish this in the fastest possible time frame, regardless of the cost.

Procuring such a large quantity of hard disks was no easy task. A team of representatives was dispatched to Southeast Asia to buy every hard disk that was available or being manufactured. This was good news for the manufacturers, but it also meant that they had to halt supplies to the manufacturers of computer systems to meet this sudden demand. There was already a backlog in the worldwide supply of hard disk drives due to the floods in Thailand, an important supply hub.

Aramco eventually had to pay higher prices to get priority supplies. A smaller company would easily have gone bankrupt in the face of such an attack. It took five months for Aramco to get its systems back in working order. As the story goes, the hackers were never identified or caught.

Aramco Cyberattack – A Timeline (Pagliery, 2015)

Unknown date	Phishing attack and intrusion
August 2012	Indications of cyberattack
15 August 2012	Over 30,000 Windows-based systems began to be overwritten; computers around the world were disconnected from the internet
August 2012	Primary enterprise systems of hydrocarbon exploration and production remain unaffected
August 2012	Manual systems in use for supplies and order fulfilment
27 August 2012	Partial recovery
January 2013	All offices set up and running online again.

Cyberattack on Iran's Nuclear Facility (2010)

The Stuxnet saga is one that demonstrates how a computer virus can bring down and cause significant *damage* even to a secure nuclear facility. Reportedly created by US and Israeli intelligence agencies to stall Iran's nuclear program, it was among the first instances of a cyberattack between countries.

Stuxnet was devised to cause physical damage to the centrifuges that Iran had deployed to enrich uranium as part of its nuclear program at the Natanz facility. The centrifuges are programmed to run at a particular speed to produce the desired results. The Stuxnet virus targeted the Programmable Logic Controllers (PLCs) that control the centrifuges and altered their speed, thereby causing irreparable damage to the centrifuges.

Stuxnet attacks work at various levels of the target infrastructure, namely the Windows and Siemens software that the PLCs were running. As the nuclear plant systems are normally air-gapped (i.e., not connected to the outside world through network connection), Stuxnet was designed to be delivered through a Universal Serial Bus (USB) stick, better known as a thumb drive. When the USB stick is connected to a machine, the virus rapidly spreads to the internal network.

The Stuxnet virus succeeded in its objective of damaging an unusually large number of centrifuges, setting Iran's nuclear program back by several years. This virus is significant because it is considered the first malware weaponised and used in an international conflict situation.

Maersk Cyberattack (2017)

NotPetya is considered one of the deadliest kinds of malware for launching *devastating* cyberattacks. The global shipping and transportation giant from Denmark, A.P. Møller-Maersk, was attacked using NotPetya on June 27, 2017. The magnitude of the attack was stupendous. Around 1,200 applications were rendered inaccessible to users, while over a 1,000 applications were destroyed. Moreover, about 3,500 servers (out of a total of 6,200 servers) and all end-user devices, including 50,000 laptops, Voice Over Internet Protocol (VOIP) phones and printers across 600 sites in 130 countries were affected and could not be reinstalled. Maersk's IT network was crippled within seven minutes, and most of the devastation was done within an hour.

The Active Directory (AD) is at the heart of modern-day systems. It is a database that holds critical information related to the IT environment, including details of users computers, and controls as well as which user is allowed access to which system and the actions they are allowed to perform. During the attack, the AD was compromised, and it took Maersk's IT Team nine days to restore its Active Directory system.

Maersk's global business involved 20 per cent of the world's trade. Their operations in the transport and logistics industries were disrupted, leading to an unprecedented impact. Container ships stood paralysed at sea, and all activities at seventy-six port terminals around the world ground to a complete halt. The potential economic impact and the adverse effect on the supply chains of companies worldwide were truly devastating.

NotPetya was named after the Petya ransomware, which could encrypt Windows machines. In the case of Petya malware, the attackers could give out a decryption key after receiving their ransom payment so that machines and data could be operational again. However, in the case of NotPetya, the malware was designed to wipe the contents on the hard disk drive and overwrite the Master Boot Record (MBR), which crashed the target machine(s) in minutes, with no hope of recovery. Hence, while Petya allowed for decryption after payment, NotPetya did not.

NotPetya was reportedly developed by the Russian military and was targeting institutions in Ukraine. However, it ended up creating collateral damage for global companies with establishments in Ukraine, such as Maersk. The attack began when an employee at Maersk responded to an email that contained the NotPetya malware.

One year before the Maersk cyberattack, Microsoft had announced the release of a software patch for a known vulnerability called EternalBlue. However, every organization (Microsoft's customers) had to update their systems with the patch provided. Organisations that were running older versions also had to update their systems to newer versions as the earlier ones were no longer supported. The spread of Petya ransomware across Europe and beyond, was attributed to unpatched systems and the EternalBlue exploit.

Another ransomware cryptoworm (worms that encrypt data) WannaCry, was quick to exploit this vulnerability (EternalBlue) and encrypted data on more than 200,000 computers across 150 countries (BBC, 2017). It is estimated that the damage caused by WannaCry ran into billions of dollars apart from the disruption it created. NotPetya came into action as the threats from WannaCry were receding by targeting the same vulnerability.

Maersk made a relatively fast recovery as they maintained back-ups of their data but suffered financial losses of up to USD 300 million, covering loss of revenue, replacement and restoration costs of damaged hardware and software and miscellaneous unexpected costs related to operations.

Maersk Cyberattack – A Timeline (Pownall, n.d.)

27 June 2017	Maersk confirms cyberattack
28 June 2017	Maersk begins response actions and confirms that the incident has been contained
29 June 2017	Maersk systems open for bookings
3 July 2017	Maersk confirms that all major IT systems have been restored
7 July 2017	Maersk reveals that it is too early to predict financial impact of the cyberattack
17 February 2018	The business disruption was estimated between $200m and $300m in lost revenues

SolarWinds Cyberattack (2019)

The SolarWinds attack is the closest to what can be termed as a *catastrophic* cyber incident. It had all the makings of such an attack. The hackers had a well-thought-out intrusion strategy to get them inside many strategic corporate and government agencies. They invested in developing a novel attack methodology via the supply chain, using a very sophisticated mode of infiltration and were prepared to cause maximum damage. The SolarWinds attack was a mega cyber event simply because the hackers' strategy was designed to trigger a much larger supply chain incident that could potentially impact thousands of organisations, including Fortune 500 companies and multiple agencies of the US government (Netzer, 2022).

The attack went undetected for several months. It was reported that the hackers might have been able to spy on a top cybersecurity firm as well as the upper echelons of the US Government. The needle of suspicion was pointed toward Russian hacking groups as it required technical expertise and organised effort to carry out such an attack. In many ways, this attack was unprecedented in its potential ability to cause widespread and massive damage.

SolarWinds is a software company founded in Tulsa, Oklahoma and headquartered in Austin, Texas. The company provides system management tools for network and infrastructure monitoring along with other technical services to its customers. In its portfolio of offerings, it also provided an IT performance monitoring system called Orion. As with other monitoring tools and systems, Orion had privileged access to an organisation's IT system to collect log files and system performance information. The hackers realised that they could infiltrate thousands of important organisations (that were customers of Orion) in one go if they could piggyback the system. According to the Security Exchange Commission (SEC) documents, SolarWinds' product Orion was used by 33,000 customers (Cimpanu, 2020). In a well-planned operation, the hackers secretly broke into the Orion system and added malicious code into an update that was to be rolled out later to all customers.

Software companies often send out software updates (patches) to add new product features or fix known bugs and issues. SolarWinds did not know that the software update it sent out in March 2020 included the malicious code planted by the hackers. The code was designed to provide a backdoor to a target organisation's IT systems. Once created, the backdoor was used as a conduit to install more malware that could enable the hackers to spy on them. This attack was named Sunburst.

Reports in the Wall Street Journal suggested that key US government establishments, including parts of the Pentagon, the Departments of Homeland Security, Energy, the State Department, the National Nuclear Security Administration and the Treasury, were attacked. It was inconceivable that some of these agencies were vulnerable for over nine months.

Among the private companies that were attacked there were big names like Microsoft, Cisco, Intel, Deloitte and even the cybersecurity firm FireEye. SolarWinds informed the SEC that up to 18,000 customers of Orion had installed the update (which had malware code in it), leaving them vulnerable and at the mercy of the hackers (Cimpanu, 2020).

Russia denied any involvement in the SolarWinds incident, even though cybersecurity experts believed they had the necessary resources to do so. Experts also opined that the true extent of damage caused by the cyberattack could never be estimated.

The SolarWinds hack was a wake-up call for the cybersecurity industry. It led to significant changes in the way software updates are designed and delivered. The motive of the hackers remains unknown even after investigation. It is also not fully clear as to what information was stolen by the hackers, if any. What is clear is that they had deep access across a range of organisations for an exceptionally prolonged period. It is also widely acknowledged that this cyber incident is one of the largest security breaches ever.

SolarWinds Attack – A Timeline (Oladimeji & Kerner, 2022)

September 2019	The hackers gain unauthorised access to the SolarWinds IT Network
October 2019	The initial test code is successfully injected into the Orion Code
February 2020	Sunburst (the malicious code) is inserted and embedded into the Orion update
March 2020	The update with the malicious code is rolled out to Orion customers
December 2020	The attack is publicly discovered and reported

The SolarWinds attack was discovered in December 2020 and rocked the cyber world with the sheer audacity of the hackers, the unprecedented tactics deployed and the potential for causing harm on a scale that could have been catastrophic.

The WEF Global Cybersecurity Outlook report from 2023 substantiates its prophecy of a cyberattack of apocalyptic proportions by highlighting the fact that the nature and scale of cybercrime are becoming increasingly unpredictable. Furthermore, it states that technology has become more destructive and refers to breakthrough technologies such as artificial intelligence. This implies that we are standing at the precipice of what can be termed a “catastrophic” cyberattack—one that will have severe and ongoing ramifications for society at large (World Economic Forum, 2023a, 2023b).

2

Dynamics of a Cyberattack

A cyberattack can be carried out in an infinite number of ways. The hackers' bag of tricks is ever-expanding, with new tactics, techniques and procedures being added every day.

Every passing year, all records regarding the amount of data lost in breaches and the number of cyberattacks on companies, governments and individuals are being broken. Whether it is increasing frequency, sophistication or the extent of damage and losses caused, cyberattacks have become a major concern for all those who rely on digital systems. To understand the dynamics of a cyberattack, we need to study the key elements that form an integral part of it. Beyond the use of technology, hackers have specific motives, strategies, tactics and easy access to an array of tools and techniques. All cyberattacks are not the same; there are those which can cause major harm, and there are those which deserve attention but cause minimal to no harm. Hence, classifying cyber incidents in terms of their severity and harm quotient can help us analyse them in their entirety and 'separate the chaff from the wheat'.

MOTIVES

For most people, the stereotypical image of the hacker is of a 'techie' with a criminal bent of mind, out to leverage technology for financial gain. They are most commonly portrayed as young men, wearing hoodies and sitting in front of their laptops, ready to carry out a cyberattack or perpetrate a scam.

However, people who have developed a greater understanding of cybercrime, know that hackers can be better portrayed and recognized based on their skill sets, motivations and affiliations.

Are all hackers or threat actors bad guys? This notion rings true for most, except the white hat hackers. These are the good guys who are aware of the way a hacker works, understand cybersecurity and specialise in finding security weaknesses and flaws. Through penetration testing and other methodologies, they help companies build strong security defences. Famous names known to have used their powers of hacking for good include Apple's Steve Wozniak, Jon Lech Johansen and Kevin Mitnick, among others.

Then there are those hackers who are bad guys, using their powers, skills and knowledge in pursuit of cybercriminal activities. Also known as threat actors, they can be categorised based on their motives and the type of hacking activities they perform.

Black hat hackers are those who are ready to perform any type of cybercriminal activity, usually for a fee. They identify vulnerabilities and weaknesses in a target IT environment and often capitalise on human errors or carelessness on the part of their victims.

White hat hackers do the same, but their intention or motive is to help organisations improve their security mechanisms based on identified vulnerabilities. White hat hackers are often hired by organisations to test the security of their networks and systems.

Another kind of hacker is an unskilled individual (*script kiddie*) who uses scripts or programs developed by others, mainly for malicious purposes like attacking networks and defacing websites. Script kiddies may also be motivated by the expectation that these acts may bring them some sort of recognition or notoriety. The easy availability of free and open-source malware can make even script kiddies launch the deadliest of attacks. Assuming that script kiddies cannot cause major damage is a fallacy, as they are good at identifying vulnerabilities and gaining access to systems. Michael Calce, a high school student from Canada, was one such script kiddie who was arrested for causing an estimated USD 1.2 billion in damage to important websites such as Yahoo, Dell, eBay and CNN (Hersher, 2015). He accomplished this by using simple tools meant for launching Denial of Service (DoS) attacks.

Hacktivists, as the name suggests, are hacker activists motivated by furthering some sort of cause, such as human rights violations, exposing wrongdoings by corporations and governments, or exacting revenge. They may also be motivated by political, social and religious agendas. Generally, hacktivists operate in groups to carry out cyberattacks. Anonymous is the name of one such group that is (in)famous for carrying out such attacks. Following the recent incursions by Russia into Ukraine, the group declared a cyber war, pulled down several Russian websites and even claimed responsibility for these attacks.

State-Sponsored Hackers or State Actors are organised groups of hackers who are 'hired' by Governments to carry out cyberattacks and espionage activities on their behalf. These groups are well-resourced with technology, people as well as required skills and have access to funding and financial support. State-sponsored hackers are known to target public utilities, corporations, defence establishments, enemy governments and even civilians. Some of the better-known groups include Cozy Bear, Lazarus Group, Double Dragon, Fancy Bear and Helix Kitten. It is alleged that Cozy Bear played a significant role in influencing the 2016 US presidential elections on behalf of the Russians (Adams, 2019).

Cybercrime syndicates are groups of hackers, programmers and other technical specialists who work together, pooling their resources to commit major cybercrimes. They are agile, organised and adept at exploiting new technologies, customising their attacks and cooperating in new ways. Hacking, fraud, development and distribution of malware, DDoS attacks, extortion and intellectual property theft are some of the cybercrimes attributed to these groups, often based on suspicion and speculation. These crime syndicates are modelled and structured along the lines of corporates. However, their focus is on gains through illegitimate cyber activities, including the sale and purchase of stolen data.

Some big names among cybercriminal syndicates are the Magecart Syndicate, Evil Corp, Dark Side and REvil. In 2018, the Magecart syndicate—specialising in hacking e-commerce platforms and stealing consumer and credit card information—breached British Airways' IT systems, compromising the personal information of their flyers. This incident affected 380,000 people.

Spy hackers are threat actors specialising in cyber spying, also known as cyber espionage. This involves the practice of obtaining classified information without the knowledge of the owner or custodian of the information using cyber tools and techniques. Spy hackers are used against various targets, including individuals, business competitors, political rivals, groups, governments and others. The objective is to obtain information that can be used as leverage and can also be a source of personal, financial, political or military advantage. Governments and corporations hire and pay these groups in return for confidential information, intelligence and trade secrets which they want regarding their competitors or enemies. Spy hackers have operated for a long time, and with changes in technology, they have more tools and techniques at their disposal today.

In 1997, Steven Davies, an engineer who worked for Gillette, stole designs of a new shaver system and sent them to Gillette's competitors via email and fax. Davis was charged with industrial espionage and sentenced to 27 months in prison. Another case of cyber espionage, known as Operation Aurora, occurred in 2010. Spy hackers attacked over twenty international companies, including Google, Adobe and Yahoo. Their aim was to steal intellectual property and trade secrets. Google attributed the incident to China and pulled out from the Chinese market. This incident raised the profile of spy hackers and was a forerunner of bigger cyber espionage incidents.

Cyber Terrorists are hackers who have a religious, political, or military agenda. They attempt to create fear and anarchy by disrupting critical infrastructures, including citizens' access to common services. They also have a wide repertoire of skills and possess the ability to carry out major attacks that can even lead to the loss of human lives. In January 2023, hackers (allegedly linked with Russia) carried out a ransomware attack on Royal Mail, the UK postal service. The attack was the handiwork of cyber terrorists who successfully disrupted the systems used to track international mail. It took over a fortnight for Royal Mail to fully restore international mail services. In the same month, in another act of cyber terrorism, hackers targeted government, military and civilian networks across the Asia Pacific. They deployed malware that could provide them access to confidential information from victims' machines as well as audio captured by infected machines' microphones.

When we think of cyber threats and attacks, we tend to think of adversaries from outside an organisation who intend to cause damage. However, the *Insider* (someone from within an organisation—employee, contractor, service provider or vendor) can be far more dangerous and cause more damage than outsiders. Most organisations focus their security efforts on attacks from the outside while even being lax regarding insider threats. The primary motivation of the malicious insider is a grievance or grouse that they have against the organisation and intends to cause damage through a data breach or cyberattack. The insider is often well-versed in the organisation's IT systems and has legitimate access to them. Awareness of security controls in place can also help in bypassing them.

Cyberattacks can also be caused by negligence of employees (*non-malicious insiders*) or errors made by them in the course of their work. During 2020, Twitter employees became the victims of phishing attacks. Hackers exploited the fact that many employees were working from home at that time. They impersonated Twitter IT administrators to gather user credentials, which they changed. Further, they gained access to administrative tools that allowed them to reset the account details of famous Twitter users, as well as change their credentials. Hacked accounts included those of Barack Obama, Elon Musk,

Bill Gates, Jeff Bezos, Michael Bloomberg, corporates like Apple, Uber and several other public personalities and companies.

A tweet from Bill Gates' official (hacked) Twitter account read, "Everyone is asking me to give back, and now is the time. I am doubling all payments sent to BTC address for the next 30 minutes. You send USD 1000, I send you back USD 2,000" (Naidu, 2020). This and other such tweets resulted in Twitter users transferring more than USD 180,000 to the scamsters' accounts. Coinbase, a cryptocurrency exchange, blocked transfers of another USD 280,000. When the news became public, Twitter's stock price fell by 4 per cent.

According to the Oxford Dictionary, a motive is "a reason for doing something, often something bad". Motives are the key drivers of action. Once they have the right motivation, hackers turn their attention to strategies for launching cyberattacks.

Targets

The first thing that happens even before formulating an attack strategy is to zero in on a target. Studies show that 86 per cent of all data breaches are financially motivated. So, for a hacker or hacker group, the value they place on the target is in terms of the money (or strategic value) that they stand to gain from carrying out the attack. For example, personal and identity information holds immense value for the hackers. They can hold it and extort money from victims, or they can sell it on the Dark Web. Businesses like financial companies, banks, retail, utilities, telecom and social media companies that store a lot of personal and sensitive information of their consumers are therefore attractive targets.

Zeroing-in

Hackers also look for targets where they can break in easily and achieve their objectives. They look for organisations which have more vulnerabilities, as well as inadequate security systems and processes in place. This is the reason why there are a greater number of attacks today on educational institutions (schools and universities), small and medium enterprises and charity organisations. While sectors like finance, utilities, manufacturing and the government have some of the most valuable data, their security is also typically of a higher order.

The following table illustrates the data sets from different industry sectors that hold value for hackers:

Banking & Financial Services	Account profiles, Know Your Customer (KYC) information, personal data, social security information, client data, credit score, credit and debit card information
Corporations–Public & Private	Employee data, customer data, contracts, financial data, intellectual property, business plans, new product information
Manufacturing Industries	Industrial designs, formulations, contracts, employee and customer data, research data
Healthcare	Patient records, billing information, clinical research data
Retail	Client information, credit and debit card information
Higher Education	Enrolment data, personal information of students and faculty, academic research, financial data, examination papers

Cybercriminals often zero in on their targets based on the effort-to-payoff ratio at play. Any sector or organisation that needs minimal effort to break in while having the potential for a payoff that meets the objectives of the hacker or hacker group is fair game for them. On the other hand, hackers also look for targets where greater efforts may be required, but there must be a guarantee that should they succeed, the chances of a large payoff are high. DarkSide, a group of hackers, targeted Colonial Pipeline, the major rich oil supplier, with a ransomware attack, knowing fully well that if their supplies were disrupted, the company would be forced to meet their ransom demand to be able to restore their supplies.

Exploiting Vulnerabilities

Large and profitable companies are also prime targets for hackers. These organisations are usually both cash-rich as well as data-rich and are lucrative targets for hackers despite the greater challenges of hacking them. These companies are better resourced and are often well organised in terms of security technology, systems, controls and processes, but they also have vulnerabilities. While organisations need to protect their systems against all types of vulnerabilities, hackers need to find only one or two vulnerabilities to launch even major attacks. Invariably, large organisations deploy a large workforce and have complex IT infrastructures that include thousands of computers, devices and applications. There are bound to be several exploitable vulnerabilities in such environments, and seasoned hackers have the means to find and exploit them.

How do hackers find vulnerabilities? The simple answer: by looking for them. Once they have identified their target, there are tools and methodologies to help hackers discover exploitable vulnerabilities.

Vulnerability scanners are a favourite tool of hackers to find and identify potential risk exposures and attack vectors across an organisation's networks, hardware, software and systems. Vulnerability scans are performed using automated vulnerability scanning tools. These tools can also help create an inventory of all IT assets (including servers, desktops, laptops, firewalls, switches, printers, etc.) connected to a network. Furthermore, for each type of IT asset, vulnerability scanners can also provide details of operating systems, software versions and open ports. Vulnerability scanners are used both by hackers (to find vulnerabilities) as well as security teams to monitor their networks, systems and applications for security vulnerabilities. Popular among vulnerability scanners are Nessus, Nexpose, OpenVAS, Nmap, Burp Suite and Wireshark.

Penetration testing is another method available to hackers to assess the security of a system against various types of attacks. The focus of the hacker here is to identify vulnerable business processes, misconfiguration, lax security controls and settings, or other weaknesses that could be exploited. The exploitability of a vulnerability means it can provide a definite path for the hacker to launch an attack.

The Common Vulnerabilities and Exposures (CVE) list is yet another source for hackers to identify vulnerabilities. This database contains all publicly known vulnerabilities and exposures, whether or not a security patch has been made available for them by the vendors concerned.

Shodan (Sentient Hyper-Optimised Data Access Network) is a useful tool for hackers to map and collate information about internet-connected devices and systems. Vulnerabilities in endpoints and IoT devices often provide hackers with opportunities to enter IT networks and launch all kinds of attacks. The Dyn DDoS attack was among the biggest ever and involved over one hundred thousand bots infected with Mirai malware (Wolfe, 2016).

The Hacker's Arsenal

A hacker is like a master craftsman in many ways. He has specific tactics, techniques and procedures (TTPs) to perform different activities that result in a cyberattack.

Tactics define the objectives and general strategies that are followed by the threat actor to execute an attack. Tactics spell out the 'how' or the 'modus operandi' of a cyberattack. Becoming a skilled hacker could mean undergoing formal hacking certification courses or learning from many websites and resources available on the internet. Many hackers join online communities, discussion groups and forums where they can exchange knowledge, techniques and software tools. Tactics adopted by hackers and hacker groups are often typical of their behaviour and can provide investigators with some clues as to who may be behind a particular cyberattack.

Techniques comprise different methods or tools that a hacker puts to use to meet his objectives. While tactics define the course of action, techniques describe the methods used by the hacker to engage in the attack, such as phishing, SQL injection attacks, cross-site scripting (XSS), etc.

Procedures relate to the step-by-step descriptions of how the hacker plans to go about achieving their objectives. Hackers, through their own learnings, develop their own 'Standard

Operating Procedures (SOPs)' for carrying out different types of attacks. Security researchers and investigators use these 'fingerprints' to identify and profile hackers and hacker groups.

Spectacularity Factor and Shock Value

A simple equation for evaluating the impact of a cyberattack is to compare the cost of effort by the hackers with the extent of loss or damage cost to the victims. When looked at in these terms, most cyberattacks which are successful will seem to be profitable ventures for the hackers. However, this equation does not fully capture the true impact of a cyberattack.

Then there is what is known as the 'spectacularity factor', which is a measure of the actual damage caused by an attack, including direct losses, loss of productivity, restoration, reputational damage and legal liability.

As per Daniel Castro, the Vice-president of the Information Technology & Innovation Foundation, a cyberattack can result in a cost ranging from USD 57 to USD 109 billion. Furthermore, he suggests that one in three businesses in the world lose all their money due to cyberattacks (Innefu Labs, n.d.).

While making money is a prime motive for conducting cyberattacks, there are some attacks that are more about making a statement, sending a message, or creating a crisis.

We are going through a phase of global economic uncertainty, which is putting great pressure on business leaders to navigate the troubled waters. They also need to be constantly aware that businesses (even mature and stable ones) can be brought down virtually overnight in the face of cyberattacks that leverage advancements in malware, artificial intelligence and other sophisticated techniques.

Even as organisations continue to deploy the best available cybersecurity solutions and improve their security processes and procedures to avoid becoming victims of a major cyberattack, there is always the lurking danger of it happening. Yet, when an attack actually happens, there is an all-pervasive sense of shock and disbelief.

The 'shock value' of a cyberattack is based on the assessment of targeted potential loss and damage following an attack. The greater the impact, the higher the shock value. Other elements of an attack that contribute to the shock value are the type of deceptive tactics (like spear phishing and stealth) used in the attack, exploitation of a known or unknown vulnerability, innovative tactics and sophistication of the attack.

Classifying a Cyber Incident

Classifying a cyber incident is important since all cyberattacks are not severe in terms of consequences, and each category of incident needs a different level of response. By doing so, incident response stakeholders can prioritise and better focus on events that matter more. We should be cognizant of the fact that categorisation may change as an investigation into the attack unfolds.

Is there a universal way of assessing a cyber incident and classifying it? While there is no single way to do this, the national security operations centre of the USA, Cybersecurity and Infrastructure Security Agency (CISA), provides a scoring system to estimate the gravity of an attack and then assign a priority to it.

The National Cyber Incident Scoring System is based on a weighted average to arrive at a score between zero and one hundred. There are eight categories representing different aspects of a cyber incident. Each category has a weight in the overall score, and the response to each category has an associated score (CISA, 2020).

The eight categories are:

Functional Impact	Location of Observed Activity	Information Impact	Cross-Sector Dependency
Observed Activity	Actor Characterisation	Recoverability	Potential Impact

Source: CISA.org

It is important to note that weights and values are specific to an individual organisation's risk assessment process. Once the incident is scored, it is assigned a priority level. The following are examples of priority codes:

Categorising a Cyber Incident (CISA, 2020)

Code	Colour Code	Description Of Incident
Emergency	**Black**	Poses an imminent threat to the provisions of wide-scale critical infrastructure
Severe	**Red**	Likely to result in a significant impact on public health or safety, national security, economic security, foreign relations, or civil liberties
High	**Orange**	Likely to result in a demonstrable impact on public health or safety, national security, economic security, foreign relations, civil liberties, or public confidence
Medium	**Yellow**	Incident may affect public health or safety, national security, economic security, foreign relations, civil liberties, or public confidence
Low	**Green**	Unlikely to affect public health or safety, national security, economic security, foreign relations, civil liberties, or public confidence.

Source: CISA.org

When we evaluate major cyberattacks that have widespread impact and those that target key industries, critical infrastructure and governments, the above scoring system is a useful way of understanding the gravity and severity of a cyber incident.

The United States Computer Emergency Readiness Team (CERT), which is a part of the Department of Homeland Security's Cybersecurity and Infrastructure Security Agency, offers a simpler methodology to categorise a cyber event. It suggests the following six categories that an entity can adopt (US-CERT, n.d).

Incident Categories

Category	Name	Description
0	**Exercise / Network Defence Testing**	Approved testing of internal/external network defences or responses by state, federal and international exercises
1	**Unauthorised access**	Anyone gaining logical or physical access without permission to a local government network, system, application, data, or other resource
2	**Denial of Service**	Any attack that successfully prevents or impairs the normal authorised functionality of networks, systems, or applications by exhausting resources. Incident includes being the victim of or participating in the Denial of Service (DoS)
3	**Malicious Code**	Successful installation of malicious software such as a virus, worm, backdoor (or other code-based malicious entity) that infects an operating system or application
4	**Improper Usage**	Anyone who knowingly or unknowingly violates acceptable computing use policies
5	**Scans/Probes/ Attempted Access**	Any activity that seeks to access or identify an entity's computer, open ports, protocols, service, or any combination for later exploit. Such an activity should not directly result in a compromise or denial of service. Cases of unauthorised internal scans are considered incidents, while most external scans are considered to be regular and, on a case-by-case basis, may warrant further investigation
6	**Investigation**	Unconfirmed incidents that could be potentially malicious or anomalous activity deemed by the reporting entity to require further review.

Source: US CERT

Once this basic categorisation is done on the type and nature of the attack, the next step is to categorise an incident based on the severity of the impact. This primarily depends on the perceived impact of the incident but is needed to determine the level and type of response required.

Incident Severity Matrix

Level	Definition	Examples
High	Incidents having a major or severe impact on operations	Includes instances of compromise of sensitive data, widespread malware attacks, unauthorised access to critical systems and Denial of Service for the entire enterprise
Medium	Incidents that have a significant impact or the potential to have a severe impact on operations	Includes small-scale Denial of Service attacks, website compromises, unauthorised access (brute force attacks against File Transfer Protocol, Secure Shell Protocol and other protocols
Low	Incidents that have a minimal impact with the potential for significant or severe impact on operations	Includes network probes or system scans, isolated virus infections or acceptable use violations

Source: CIS Centre for Internet Security

Incident Scoping, Reporting and Response

Scoping an incident is a critical component of the overall response process. Such an exercise involves identifying potential targets (e.g., known compromised systems, possibly affected systems, important systems), determining the external touch points (e.g., internet, wireless, third party and remote access connections), and figuring out probable scenarios (e.g., internal vs external threat, targeted attack vs opportunistic attack and visualising data and traffic flows).

With an increasing number of cyberattacks happening and their possible widespread ramifications, incident reporting is critical. It not only enables the victim organisation to learn from the incident but also allows for others from the same industry or geography as they could be the next targets. Countries around the world have developed their own mandates when it comes to the nature, content and documentation required, as well as sector-specific mandates, guidelines and timelines. For instance, in the US, covered entities are required to report to CISA any cyber incidents within 72 hours from the time the entity reasonably believes the incident occurred (CISA, n.d). Similarly, the European Union (EU) in 2018 introduced notification rules for cybersecurity incidents for operators of essential services in a wide range of critical (ENISA, 2022) sectors, such as energy, transport, finance and health. In India, the Computer Emergency Response Team (CERT-In) issued directions in April 2022 relating to information security practices, procedures, prevention, response and reporting of cyber incidents. Under the directive, any service provider, intermediary, data centre, corporate and government organisation has to compulsorily report cyber incidents to CERT-In within 6 hours of discovering such incidents to be reported. The type of incidents have also been specified and include incidents involving targeted scanning, probing of critical networks, identity theft, phishing, data breach, data leaks, unauthorised access of IT systems, defacement of website or intrusion into a website and unauthorised changes such as inserting malicious code, links to external websites, etc. (Niketan, 2022).

It is important to note that as the investigation of a cyber incident proceeds, new information emerges, which may lead to the reclassification of the incident and may require rescoping.

All cyber incidents, regardless of how severe they may be, warrant a series of steps to be taken to enable recovery and implement additional security measures to prevent future attacks. A structured incident response process is based on the following predetermined steps and course of action. The National Institute of Standards and Technology (NIST) breaks down the incident response process into the following steps (Scarfone et al., 2008):

- *Preparation* – This involves the creation of a plan to prevent and respond to events. The plan must clearly indicate who is responsible for each activity, as well as who has the authority to make certain critical decisions. Preparation must also include the acquisition of technological tools, skills and personnel who will be a part of the incident response process.
- *Detection and Analysis* – This step involves the precursors and indicators of an incident, conducting an analysis of them, documenting, prioritising and notifying all those who need to know.
- *Containment, Eradication and Recovery* – This is a critical step of the process that involves the development of a strategy for containment, eradication and recovery. Important considerations are the importance of the affected assets and systems, the severity of the incident and the impact on business processes. Documentation is an essential activity that is important throughout the process to capture learning from incidents as well as to collect evidence which may be useful in evaluating future incidents as well as for potential litigation.
- *Post-Incident Activity* – It is important that all stakeholders in the incident come together to document lessons from all major incidents and contribute to retaining learnings from less severe incidents, which may be useful in improving security as a whole and incident handling.

The Long Tail

As the initial shock of a major cyberattack fades, several issues related to its aftermath come to the fore. For one thing, it is never going to be business as usual for the organisation again. Security issues take centre stage. While all levels of management begin to grapple with immediate issues such as restoring IT systems, getting business back on track, determining the losses and costs and handling media and other external agencies, there are even more critical issues that need to be dealt with in the longer term.

Consider this: the average time to resolve a data breach was 277 days in 2022, while the average time to resolve a destructive attack was 324 days. The average cost of a data breach caused by a ransomware attack is USD 4.54 million, while the average cost of a destructive attack is USD 5.12 million (Ermetic, 2022).

Most often, the costs of suffering a cyberattack end up being greater than what is initially estimated. Expeditors International of Washington, Inc., which is among the largest logistics companies globally, was hit by a cyberattack on February 20, 2022 (Liu, 2022). While the company did not confirm that it was a ransomware attack, their immediate actions of shutting down all billing and accounting systems in order to protect their data seemed to point towards this. This action also stopped its activities of shipping, customs processing, and distributing customer products for three weeks.

The company had to spend USD 20 million on investigating, remediating and recovering from the cyberattack, in addition to the lost business of about USD 40 million. To add to their woes, they did not have any cyber insurance. Just when they thought they had wrapped up all issues related to the cyberattack, iRobot, one of their long-standing customers whose shipments were affected due to the cyberattack, slapped them with a lawsuit as they had to incur extraordinary costs as Expeditors could not adhere to their contractual terms. The lawsuit calls for Expeditors to pay iRobot USD 2.1 million plus interest at 9 per cent and legal fees. The two parties have scheduled a meeting in February 2024 to reach a final settlement a full two years after the attack happened (Barner, 2023).

The long tail in terms of both actions and costs can extend beyond months to several years, and in this period, lead the victim organisation to meet several unbudgeted expenses. In terms of costs, reports suggest that the long tail could mean incurring 67 per cent of costs in the first year, 22 per cent in the second year, and 11 per cent in the third year (Mclean, 2023).

Cyberattacks can adversely impact and cost an organisation in ways that will vary depending on the nature and severity of the event. The only positive that an organisation can take forward after a cyberattack are the learnings which can help them avoid future cyberattacks, or at the very least, limit the damage caused in case they face another.

Dr Christopher Frei, Secretary of the World Energy Council, has said, "We are in the stone age of cyber security. Real learning will only come after the 1st major incident"(McArthur, 2017). Cyberattacks can be an important source of learning. Losing lessons learned is a lost opportunity. Maersk CEO Soren Skou said, based on his experience, that "Until you have experienced something like this, you don't realise just what can happen, just how serious it can be" (Financial Times, n.d).

3

Types of Cyberattacks: The Hackers' Dirty Dozen

There are a thousand ways to skin a cat, it is said. Similarly, there are a thousand ways in which cyberattacks can be launched.

To better understand how cyberattacks are conducted by hackers, we must examine their strategies, approaches and methodologies. A cyberattack can be launched from any location. It can be performed by an individual or a group using one or more strategies, methodologies and approaches. The hackers' arsenal comprises today of a variety of basic tools, techniques and procedures (TTPs) that can be used to exploit vulnerabilities in computer systems and networks as well as some advanced techniques that can cause the maximum amount of damage and even mayhem in a target organisation or IT environment. The 'hackers' dirty dozen' is a compilation of the types of attacks that currently are at the top of the hackers' billboard charts.

Cyberattacks can be categorised as active or passive attacks. Active attacks are attempts to modify system resources or impact their operation, while passive attacks are those that attempt to learn or leverage information from the system without impacting its system resources.

Active and Passive Attacks – Examples

Active Attacks	**Passive Attacks**
DDOS Attacks	Computer and Network Surveillance
Spoofing	Port Scanning

Contd.

Network Attacks	Wire Tapping
Buffer, Stack Overflow	Keystroke Logging *Contd.*
SQL Injection (where the database is altered)	SQL Injection (where the database information is exposed)
Phishing	Man in the Middle
Session Hijacking	Foot Printing
Mixed Threat Attacks	Dumpster Diving

Cyberattacks aim to cause damage to a resource (logical or physical) by exploiting one or more vulnerabilities. In some cyberattacks, the damage caused may relate to theft or exposure of sensitive data or comprise the confidentiality, integrity, or availability of the targeted resource. The key to launching attacks is the identification of vulnerabilities and the use of tools and techniques that enable cybercriminals to exploit them.

Malware Attacks

Malware is an umbrella term that covers a wide variety of software that acts as a primary weapon in the hands of hackers to launch cyberattacks. Malware of any kind is software that is intended to cause disruption and damage to a target computer, server, or network.

Everyday over half a million new pieces of malware are discovered. This is not surprising since seventeen million new malware instances are registered every month. Overall, there are over a billion malware programs in cyberspace at present. Furthermore, four companies are attacked every minute (Craft, 2023). The most dangerous forms of malware include viruses, worms, trojans, adware, backdoors, rootkits, spyware and ransomware.

A malware attack can be detected by close observation of some tell-tale signs, including slowing down, hanging or crashing of systems, browser redirects, changes in system configuration, disappearing data files and strange pop-ups. Although firewalls and antivirus software play a major role in blocking malware attacks, it is still possible that newer forms of malware can get past existing protections and controls, given that over 3,50,000 new malware codes are being released everyday (Vigderman & Gabe, 2023).

Viruses and Worms

Viruses and worms can be deadly and have the potential to cause extreme damage to both data and software. They both can self-replicate and spread quickly. The two terms are often used interchangeably but have one major difference, namely that viruses must be triggered by the activation of their host computer, whereas worms are stand-alone malicious programs that need no external activation and propagate across a network on their own.

12 Deadliest Viruses and Worms

ILOVEYOU	Zeus
WannaCry	Sobig
Klez	Slammer
Cryptolocker	CodeRed
Stuxnet	Tanatos/Bugbear
Mirai	Flashback

The ILOVEYOU virus (actually a worm) is among the earliest instances of malware causing widespread damage. In 2000, when the world was just recovering from the Y2K problem that was expected to cause havoc in the digital world, the ILOVEYOU virus caused havoc by sending a phony "love letter" through what seemed to be a harmless file. ILOVEYOU was designed to send copies of itself to all the email addresses that appeared in the contact list of an infected machine. Very soon, it went on to infect over ten million personal computers around the world.

In 2004, Mydoom, a similar worm, created an estimated damage of USD 38 billion. Mydoom was also capable of integrating an infected machine into a botnet (a network of computers infected with malware that are controlled by a bot herder)that launched Distributed Denial of Services (DDoS) attacks. Zeus, a Trojan horse malware, caused billions of dollars of losses by mounting attacks on over 2,000 organisations and 76,000 computers in 196 countries. The Sobig worm in 2003 spread like wildfire and infected millions of internet-connected Microsoft Windows computers. In a short period, the economic damage caused by Sobig rose to USD 14.62 billion as reports surfaced of millions of organisations and households worldwide being infected. It was reported at that time that the economic damage was a world record earlier held by Klez (Help Net Security, 2003). Klez worm (2001), like Sobig, had the ability to randomly pick email addresses from an infected computer and propagate itself to other systems. Klez is considered among the most destructive worms in history, having caused damage worth nearly USD 13.92 billion.

Common Types of Computer Viruses

Boot Sector Virus	Web Scripting Virus	Polymorphic Virus
Browser Hijacker	File Infector Virus	Multipartite Virus
Resident Virus	Direct Action Virus	Macro Virus

Rootkits are yet another form of malware that enables hackers to gain access to and exfiltrate data from machines while remaining undercover. While it is common to hear about viruses that are used to attack machines using Windows OS, Machiavelli was the first rootkit targeted at the Mac OS X. The ZeroAccess botnet was created from a rootkit and was designed to consume system resources while mining for Bitcoin. The botnet had nearly two million machines. Variants of ZeroAccess are available even now and are active.

A Trojan horse is a program that is designed to deceive by seeming to be useful for performing a specific function while they are actually performing a malicious function. There are various types of Trojans, such as backdoors, downloaders, DDoS attack Trojans and Rootkit Trojans. Each is designed with a view to get the hacker into a system or network and then take control of different resources. The Zeus/Zbot is an example which hackers used to infect 3.6 million computers in the USA, including machines owned by the US Department of Transportation, National Space & Aeronautical Agency

(NASA) and the Bank of America. Endpoint security, as well as web application firewalls, are useful to enhance defences against Trojans (Imperva, n.d.).

Ransomware Attacks

A ransomware attack is one of the most dreaded forms of cyberattack. It has both a high shock quotient and usually a significant harm quotient. A ransomware attack could potentially impact the key business systems of an organisation, paralysing its operations and affecting the entire value chain of which the organisation is a part. The first known instance of ransomware was the "AIDS Trojan", which was created by Joseph Popp way back in 1989. It did not have the expected outcome (ransom payment) due to a design failure. Since then, ransomware has come a long way, and today, it has risen to the prime position of being the most common form of malware. The lure of earning money by extorting large sums of money, combined with the minimum risk of getting caught, has made ransomware attacks attractive for cybercriminals. Key sectors that have been targeted by ransomware attacks include (but are not limited to) legal firms, financial services companies, critical infrastructure and manufacturing organisations. Management teams of organisations affected by ransomware are confronted with Hobson's Choice (apparently free choice where there is no real alternative) of paying the ransom so that their systems are unlocked, and they can proceed with their business operations. Since sudden and unplanned non-availability of systems like billing and accounting have an adverse impact on the credibility and reliability of a business enterprise, payment of ransom offers a way out. Organisations affected by ransomware can potentially suffer massive losses in terms of money and, in the longer term, a loss of customers and even employees.

Ransomware attacks also are often well-planned by hackers and follow a specific sequence. A typical sequence of a ransomware attack starts with the attacker running probing scans to identify vulnerabilities in a network and the devices connected to it. Other ways of starting a ransomware attack are through malware infections, phishing, drive-by downloads and exploiting other identified vulnerabilities. Once the malware payload is delivered into an organisation's network and is activated, important mission-critical, business-critical systems and other files are encrypted and become unavailable for users, thereby disrupting operations. What follows is a ransomware demand, often payable in cryptocurrency. The attackers will release the decrypting key on the receipt of the ransom or even sometimes proceed to expose stolen data in underground markets even though a ransom has been paid. The hackers could even make additional ransom demands; hence, there is no real guarantee of regaining access to the data or getting any assurance that it will not be exposed.

A global study done by Sophos, a security company, in 2021 found that less than ten per cent of organisations surveyed recovered all data after paying a ransom, and less than a third were able to recover half the data (Cook, 2023).

The WannaCry ransomware in 2017 caused widespread damage across 150 countries, infecting over 200,000 computers. The losses on account of WannaCry attacks are estimated at a whopping USD 4 billion. The attack ranks high on the shock quotient since, apart from businesses and government organisations, even hospitals were targeted. The National Health Services (NHS) of the UK, which was one of the organisations targeted, could not handle new patients and emergencies in the absence of access to health data that was encrypted by the attackers. Again, in 2020, one of the potentially largest ransomware attacks in medical history hit a US hospital chain, Universal Health Services. The groups' hospitals across more than 400 locations were compelled to cancel scheduled surgeries. They had to make use of paper records to keep their operations going.

The US Treasury, in a finding, has linked more than USD 5 billion of Bitcoin transactions to ransomware (Cook, 2023). Organisations that did not pay the ransom have no option but to rebuild their systems from scratch. Those that have up-to-date backups had fewer problems in doing so and recovering from an attack.

Over the years, ransomware has become more refined and specialised. Given below is a list of different variants of ransomware.

Crypto Ransomware or Encryptors	Encrypts files and data within a system and prevents users from accessing them. Requires decryption key for recovery of data.
Scareware	A ransomware that can flood screens with pop-up alerts with or without actually locking or damaging files.
Doxware or Leakware	Leakware warns that the hackers will expose sensitive personal or company information online. This is designed to make people panic and pay the ransom lest their information falls into the hands of cybercriminals or is posted in the public domain. Doxing is a form of cyberbullying which uses sensitive or confidential information that can cause harassment and financial harm to targeted individuals or organisations.
Lockers	As the name suggests, this type of ransomware locks users out of a system and renders both files and applications inaccessible. A ransom demand is displayed on the screens, along with a countdown clock to pressurise victims to pay the ransom.
RaaS (Ransomware as a Service)	RaaS is malware made available on demand by hosted service providers who enable hackers to 'hire' the software to launch a ransomware attack, including all aspects of the attack, such as distributing ransomware, receiving payments and restoring access, in return for a share of the ransom.

There are various types of ransomware, some of which are more popular than other variants for specific purposes. When it comes to simply encrypting and exfiltrating files, there are popular ransomware like Teslacrypt, Lockbit, CryptoWall, WannCry and NotPetya. Ransomware like Revil, also known as Sodinokibi, while performing basic functions like encrypting and exfiltrating data, can also delete the ransom demand message after infection. Messages typically ask that ransom payments must be made in bitcoin, and if not made in time, the ransom would be double of what was initially demanded.

Cryptolocker, another popular ransomware, caused enormous damage, causing USD 665 million in losses across over 5,000 organisations and infecting over 250,000 computers. Cerber is an example of Ransomware as a Service, which makes it easier for hackers to launch attacks with minimal technical skills and low upfront investment.

Defeating the motives of ransomware attacks involves organisations installing basic security measures like firewalls, antivirus, implementing zero trust, endpoint security, network segmentation, email protection and limiting user privileges. Another important measure is to maintain up-to-date backups, which can be used to recover from a ransomware attack. Such backups should also be maintained on air-gapped systems or offline to prevent hackers from infecting them, too.

Password Cracking and Brute Force Attacks

Brute force attacks are trial-and-error attempts to guess usernames, passwords, credentials and encryption keys to gain access to a system. In the context of database security, such attacks can cause a lot of damage if successful. Reportedly, over fifty per cent of hackers like to use brute force attacks to exploit cloud architecture's vulnerabilities, such as misconfigured software or easily gettable admin usernames (Magnusson, 2023). Advanced forms of brute force attacks include dictionary attacks, where a big list of passwords is used by running a brute force program script, or credential stuffing, wherein the hacker already has knowledge of a username and password combination for one system and uses the same to access other accounts of the same user.

In 2015, Dunkin' Donuts suffered a brute force attack that resulted in hackers getting access to nearly 20,000 user accounts and stealing their money. The company did not inform the concerned users and had to pay USD 650,000 to settle lawsuits filed against them. In 2016, Alibaba, the e-commerce giant, faced a brute force attack where 21 million user accounts were compromised. It was later revealed that most users were using the same passwords for other accounts or weak passwords that could be cracked easily (Magnusson, 2023) .

While the responsibility of safeguarding user data that is held by an enterprise or organisation rests with them, users must also exercise care and caution in selecting passwords that are not easy to break and should use different passwords for different accounts.

Database Attacks

Database attacks can result in instances of data theft, data destruction and data manipulation. Databases are among the most targeted information assets as they hold large amounts of sensitive data. Database attacks are hard to detect, though it takes an average of ten seconds for a skilful hacker to get in and out of a database (Higgins Jackson Kelly, 2008). Database attacks can happen due to misconfiguration, use of weak passwords, and failure to update Operating Systems (OS) and software versions apart from other vulnerabilities. It is a good cybersecurity practice to encrypt all sensitive data, as missing encryption or the use of poor encryption techniques could result in the exposure of sensitive data and cause major damage.

Hackers today are adept at stealing data, which is not only 'at rest' but also 'in transmission', using packet sniffing techniques that enable them to capture network packets and intercept or pilfer data that may be unencrypted. Privilege escalation is another method where attackers, after obtaining access to a user account, bypass authorisation protocols and grant themselves access, user rights and privileges to cause further damage.

Common Database Attacks

SQL injection attacks	Brute force attacks	Packet sniffing
Privilege escalation	Missing or poor encryption	Unprotected backups

SQL injection (SQLi) attacks occur where the fields available for user input let SQL statements through to query the database directly. SQL stands for Structured Query Language, which is used for updating or retrieving data from a database. SQLi attacks enable hackers to modify, alter, delete and manipulate database information, as well as to access and recover files. The 7-Eleven retail chain data breach is an example of an SQLi attack which facilitated hackers in stealing 130 million credit card numbers. Database attacks are not new and have resulted in massive data breaches with enormous adverse consequences for the victims, including financial losses, damage to reputation and lawsuits.

Top database breaches along with the number of records compromised:

Year	Organisation	Number of records compromised/stolen
2012	**LinkedIn**	117 million emails and passwords
2013	**Yahoo**	Three billion accounts, including names, birth dates, phone numbers, security questions and passwords of users that were encrypted.
2013	**MySpace**	Around 360 million, including account information
2013	**Adobe**	Usernames and encrypted passwords from nearly 38 million active accounts
2014	**eBay**	145 million theft of names, email addresses and other personal data of eBay customers
2014	**Home Depot**	Data pertaining to 56 million cards
2017	**Equifax**	Private records of 147.9 million Americans, 15.2 million British citizens and about 19,000 Canadian citizens
2018	**Marriott**	Up to 500 million guest records
2019	**Facebook**	Over 533 million Facebook users from 106 countries

Database security requires the implementation of several best practices, such as assessing and fixing vulnerabilities, careful management of user rights and privileges, blocking malicious web requests, encrypting sensitive data, maintaining (online and offline) backups and monitoring database access activity. Since weak passwords are one of the causes that lead to a data breach, employees must be sensitised to use strong passwords and identify common cyber threats.

Phishing and Social Engineering

The first foothold for a cyber attacker is to obtain sensitive information such as usernames, passwords, credit card details or any information that could help provide an entry into a target account. Phishing is the act of deceiving potential victims to part with such information by using emails, phone calls or text messages. Social engineering is a broader term that includes phishing and other methods, using psychological manipulation on targeted victims to get them to make security mistakes or give away sensitive information. Other forms of social engineering include baiting, using scareware and pretexting. The word 'scam' is appropriate to describe instances of large-scale social engineering. In today's digital world, scams abound. Deception is an important component of phishing and social engineering campaigns, where the idea is to appear legitimate, trusted, or harmless while harbouring malicious intentions.

Studies on phishing emails reveal surprising numbers: nearly 1.2 per cent of all emails sent are malicious, which translates to 3.4 billion phishing emails daily. Another staggering statistic suggests that over one-third of all data breaches involved phishing, according to Verizon's 2022 report (James, 2023).

Business Email Compromise (BEC) fraud is among the social engineering schemes that can often result in monetary losses. A BEC attack (also known as Email Account Compromise or CEO impersonation) is a thriving business for hackers today. After researching a target to identify those executives who can undertake wire transfers, such as accountants and the CFO, the hacker typically sends a mail from the CEO or a person of similar authority, asking to transfer a sum of money to a particular account urgently for some seemingly important purpose. Since the person transferring the money believes that the email has come from an appropriate authority demanding urgent action, they do not exercise caution and may even bypass regular checks and balances to initiate the money transfer.

A variation of a BEC attack is the use of invoices generated on an organisation's letterhead, which, though having proper transaction information such as order number, items ordered and price (stolen by gaining control of email accounts), are actually fake. The fake invoice is sent with a request that there has been a change in their bank account and that payment should be remitted to a new bank account number, which is, in fact, controlled by the hackers.

The magnitude of these attacks and their success rate can be gauged from the arrest of a three-member BEC scammer group that stole nearly 11 million Euros by the Spanish Civil Guard as a part of Operation Lavanco. The group had cast its net wide, covering businesses from 12 countries, including Belgium, Bulgaria, the USA, the UK, Venezuela, Norway, Germany, Luxembourg, Portugal and Chile.

In 2018, another operation was conducted by US agencies (Operation reWired), which was targeted against BEC scammers, and 281 people were arrested from all over the world.

The FBI's Internet Crime Complaint Centre announced that 166,349 complaints of BEC incidents were received (both domestic and international) between June 2016 and July 2019, with a total estimated loss of more than USD 26 billion (Gatlan, 2019).

There are many more variants of BEC that hackers use, such as attorney impersonation, tax authorities' impersonation, etc. Preventing such attacks is challenging as it calls for a high degree of situational awareness among staff, robust vendor processes and authorisation, checks and balances relating to money transfers where more than one person is in control, taking due care when urgent requests or change requests are made, and checking through other methods like phone calls or face-to-face meetings before initiating payments.

There are other social engineering and spear phishing scenarios that attempt to steal passwords by impersonating customer care, IT admin and insurance agents who send authentic-looking communications to trap people into exposing their personal information and credentials. In 2019, CNBC reported that fraudsters conned Facebook and Google out of more than USD 100 million between 2013 and 2015, citing the US Attorney's Office for the Southern District of New York.

Evaldas Rimasauskas incorporated a company that impersonated another company, Taiwan-based Quanta Computer, which did business with Facebook and Google. He had full control of the fake company and opened bank accounts in Latvia and Cyprus. Rimasauskas and his associates crafted and sent fake invoices on behalf of Quanta (which seemed genuine to employees at Facebook and Google), who went ahead and paid out more than USD 100 million to the fake company's bank accounts. Eventually, Rimasauskus was arrested in 2017 by Lithuanian authorities and extradited to the US, where he was sentenced to a 30-year prison sentence. He also had to forfeit approximately USD 50 million from his ill-gotten money (Huddleston, 2019). There is really no substitute for awareness and alertness when it comes to dealing with such attacks. Certainly, one to watch out for both organisations and individuals.

Web Attacks

Web attacks, as a category, include various types of attacks that are targeted towards a website or web applications. These include attacks such as Cross Site Scripting, SQL injection (which was covered under database attacks), Session Hijacking, DDoS attacks, as well as malware attacks. As is evident, attack techniques overlap over what is categorised as 'the dirty dozen' attack vectors, as hackers use multiple techniques across attack vectors to achieve their objectives.

In 2011, it was found that hackers were using two out of three discovered cross site scripting (XSS) vulnerabilities in a period of ten days to launch attacks on Facebook users. The first issue came to light on the mobile version, where the interface was prompting users to post stories on the user's wall, while in the second, viral links were included to distribute malware or phishing links. The third XSS issue was related to a channel page on Facebook for session management, where injected code altered the behaviour of the page. Once these were discovered, Facebook went ahead and resolved the issues. Again, in 2020, a security researcher Vinoth Kumar earned USD 20,000 as a 'bug-bounty' by finding an XSS vulnerability that affected the 'Login with Facebook' button (Leyden John, 2020).

XSS is a client-side code injection attack where the attacker executes malicious code in a webpage or web application. Other vulnerable areas which are used to launch XSS attacks are blogs, forums, bulletin boards and web pages that allow comments. Prevention of XSS attacks involves not allowing inputs from unknown sources, as well as parsing user inputs and validating them at the browser level before a script is executed.

In 2020, when the world was battling COVID-19, the use of video conferencing platforms was at its peak. A series of 'Zoom-bombings' were reported as hijackers found ways to intrude on video calls and display unwanted and undesirable messages and even porn. These uninvited 'guests' exploited the web session control mechanism to hijack an ongoing session. A session hijacking assault or a Transmission Control Protocol session hijacking attack takes place when an attacker assumes command over a client's session. After a spate of such attacks, web conference platforms, including Zoom, tightened their security controls.

Distributed Denial of Service (DDoS) Attacks

On October 21, 2016, three successive DDoS attacks brought about what was then the biggest DDoS attack in history. The attack was so disruptive that users in North America and Europe could not access major internet platforms for several hours. A look at the platforms affected reads like a who's-who of the internet world: Airbnb, Amazon.com, Ancestry.com, The A.V. Club, BBC, The Boston Globe, Box, Business Insider, CNN, Comcast, CrunchBase, DirecTV, Electronic Arts, Etsy, FiveThirtyEight, Fox News, The Guardian, GitHub, Grubhub, HBO, Imgur, Mashable, National Hockey League, Netflix, The New York Times, Overstock.com, PayPal, Pinterest, Pixlr,

PlayStation Network, Qualtrics, Quora, Reddit, Roblox, Second Life, Shopify, Slack, SoundCloud, Squarespace, Spotify, Starbucks, Storify, Swedish Civil Contingencies Agency, Swedish Government, Tumblr, Twilio, Twitter, Verizon Communications, Visa, Vox Media, Walgreens, The Wall Street Journal, Wikia, Wired, Wix.com, WWE Network, Xbox Live, Yammer and more (Helmke Mathew, 2019).

The strategies, tactics and weapons used in this attack make for a unique construct designed for maximum impact. Two groups, Anonymous and New World Hackers, claimed responsibility for the attack, but no evidence was provided to support the claim. The hackers strategically targeted the Domain Name System (DNS) servers, which were hosted by DYN, one of the leading providers of DNS services. DNS servers function as one would use a telephone directory in yesteryears to locate a telephone number. In the internet world, DNS servers translate a domain name, which is typed into an Internet Protocol (IP) address—a unique numerical identifier assigned to every device or network that connects to the internet. DNS servers help in both identifying and locating computer systems and resources on the internet. All the organisations listed above were users of DNS services provided by DYN.

The weapon used was the Mirai botnet, which was among the largest botnets in the history of the internet. Most botnets are made up of computers, but Mirai had all kinds of Internet of Things (IoT) devices, like cameras, printers, routers, DVR players and even baby monitors, which were then infected with the Mirai malware. In December 2017, Paras Jha, Josiah White and Dalton Norman pleaded guilty to crimes related to the Mirai botnet. They were students in the age group of 18-25 when they created a digital army in the form of the Mirai botnet. The trio was convicted and sentenced to 2,500 hours of community service, confinement and fines. This one-of-its-kind attack had an extraordinary attack strength of 1.2 Terabytes per second and involved up to a hundred thousand endpoints (Woolf, 2015).

Thousands of legitimate users suffered due to the outage caused by the sheer volume of traffic that was generated by the botnet and bombarded the DYN servers until they could not perform their defined functions. Botnets grow because of users' and administrators' use of default, reused or weak passwords. Patching software and firmware on time and minimising the attack surface are other ways of reducing the chances of a DDoS attack.

Insider Threats

Most organisations direct their cybersecurity efforts and controls towards threats originating from outside the organisation. While it is true that more threats emanate from external sources, insider threats can also be potentially devastating. An insider is anyone who is an employee (both current and past), contractor, vendor, service provider, consultant, business partner, associate or board member who has access to an organisation's systems and data. Insiders have legitimate access to an organisation's system, making it very difficult to prevent such attacks. They are also privy to the 'lay of the land' and have knowledge about valuable information assets and where they are available. They could also be aware of vulnerabilities and weaknesses in security controls in place.

Boeing, the aerospace giant, suffered an instance of the longest insider threat attacks, extending from 1979 to 2006. A Boeing employee was eventually caught, but the overall scope of data stolen (which could have covered information about space programs and military manufacturing) could not be established. It was alleged that the insider may have been working for Chinese intelligence (Exabeam, n.d.).

Insiders are also likely to be hired by competitors to steal intellectual property, which they can use to their advantage. In the technology world, it takes years of effort and millions of dollars to develop intellectual property, which may have great value and earn them a strong position in the market. Apple, considered by many as the most innovative technology company, filed a lawsuit in April 2022 against a tech startup called Rivos. It alleged that Rivos hired forty ex-Apple employees, of which two engineers were accused of stealing Security Operations Centre (SoC) information that was useful for developing a system-on-chip SoC technology solution (Simpson, 2022).

Proofpoint, a leading cybersecurity company, reported that, on average, impacted organisations spend USD 15.4 million annually to remediate threats emanating from negligent, compromised and malicious insiders. Furthermore, the report suggests that it took 85 days to contain each incident (ISBUZZ Staff, 2022).

Another sensational case that rocked the internet world was discovered in May 2022. A senior research scientist at Yahoo, Qian Sang, stole 570,000 files containing source code, architecture information, proprietary algorithms and other intellectual property (IP) information related to a product called Adlearn. It was later revealed that Sang had received a job offer from one of Yahoo's competitors. Yahoo went on to file three charges against Sang, including one for IP theft. Insiders, due to their privileged position, can cause major damage to organisations, especially in the context of IP theft (Clark, 2022).

Among important preventive measures against insider attacks, organisations are increasingly turning to zero-trust approaches, which treat insiders on par with outsiders, ensuring that they follow authentication protocols. Along with this, it is important to ensure that off-boarding processes are strictly followed when an employee leaves an organisation and monitoring user access to sensitive information. Monitoring systems can enable real-time analysis of user behaviour and raise warning signals after identifying unusual or suspicious activities. It is important to recognise that not all insiders have malicious intent, and that negligence or a lack of awareness can also cause exposure of sensitive data. Security awareness training must be an ongoing component of all security efforts, and due attention must be given to this aspect.

Network Attacks

Breaking into a network is a major step in launching a cyberattack. IT networks today are highly complex, with a plethora of hardware systems and devices, software, services, communication protocols, virtual resources and users. Furthermore, the network perimeter, as it existed some years ago, has changed from being fixed to flexible. Users of IT networks can connect from anywhere, whereas earlier, they could connect only from office locations. Remote working is part and parcel of a modern-day enterprise, and the network boundary extends to wherever the user logs in from. The migration to cloud-based systems has also redefined network boundaries from being within the four walls of a data centre to virtually anywhere. All this poses huge challenges when it comes to securing networks from cyberattacks.

Hackers use a variety of attack vectors to launch network attacks, including DDoS attacks, DNS spoofing, IP spoofing, MiTM, Rootkits, endpoint vulnerabilities, malware attacks, zero-day attacks and privilege escalation. In short, exploiting any system vulnerability can serve as an entry point for a hacker to gain unauthorised access into a network and thereafter use advanced techniques to cause disruption and damage. As we have dealt with some of the attack vectors earlier in this chapter, we will examine other vectors such as Domain Name System (DNS) Spoofing, Privilege Escalation, Cloud computing, Endpoint attacks and threats arising from remote working.

In simple terms, DNS is the internet equivalent of a telephone directory, which routes web addresses and connects web browsers with websites. In a DNS attack, the threat actor uses rigged DNS server data to redirect users to spurious websites. These fake websites are designed to resemble legitimate websites so that users unknowingly part with sensitive data. In 2018, hackers compromised Amazon's Route 53 DNS server and public Google DNS servers, thereby redirecting nearly 1,300 IP addresses which were craftily designed to steal user credentials and other information. MyEtherWallet, a cryptocurrency website, was one of their key targets, where during a two-hour attack window, they stole USD 152,000 (Panda Media Centre, 2022). Using secure connections, VPNs and antivirus software, and not falling prey to suspicious links can help prevent such attacks.

Privilege escalation is an important part of a cyberattack sequence, where after gaining unauthorised access to a network, attackers aim to gain access to accounts that have greater privileges (i.e. permissions to perform more actions, including configuration and granting permissions). Typically, a system administrator's privileges and powers go beyond an ordinary system user. The attacker wants to use these privileges to misconfigure systems, manipulate system security controls and grant privileges to new accounts which are under his control to deploy new payloads. Through privilege escalation, attackers gain elevated rights that enable them to open multiple doors through which they can deploy other attack vectors. Commonly used techniques to launch privilege escalation attacks include Windows Sticky Keys, and Metasploit, which is used for information gathering in a target environment. While Metasploit is the most popular penetration testing tool which enables the discovery of weaknesses in system defences, in the wrong hands, it can be used for privilege escalation. Another technique used by hackers is to bypass user account control mechanisms and manipulate access tokens.

Network attacks can be disruptive and may result in unplanned downtime. With ninety-eight per cent of global organisations migrating to cloud-based systems, hackers have also upped their game and capabilities in attacking networks where organisations use cloud services. It is, therefore, not surprising that there was a forty-eight per cent year-on-year jump in cyberattacks on cloud-based networks, according to Check Point, a leader in cybersecurity solutions (Burt, n.d.).

Cloud systems that generally have better levels of security also have their share of vulnerabilities. Common among them are misconfiguration, vulnerable access management and Application Programming Interfaces (APIs). In August 2021, Accenture, the IT services and consulting giant, became a victim of a ransomware attack, where hackers stole 6 Terabytes of data and demanded a ransom of USD 50 million. The needle of suspicion pointed to the LockBit group, which provides Ransomware-as-a-Service to hackers who want to perform ransomware attacks. Accenture, while admitting the attack on their network, said that no customer systems were affected. The hackers, on their part, were reported to have dumped the stolen data online when they failed to get the ransom demanded (Nicholas, 2021).

The endpoints of a network are entry points for hackers. An endpoint is any remote computing device that connects to a network, such as servers, desktops, laptops, tablets, mobile phones, IoT devices and appliances. The list of endpoints is continuously growing, and considering the fact that they are extremely vulnerable to various kinds of cyberattacks, this is indeed scary. Further, the shift to remote working models has made corporate IT environments more complex and networks more vulnerable since a variety of devices connect to them from outside traditional security borders. According to IBM's 'Cost of a Data Breach' report (2021), the shift to remote working has already cost businesses over a million dollars due to data breaches (Dragonetti, n.d.). Common endpoint attacks are in the form of phishing, malware, cryptojacking and DDoS attacks. To counter endpoint threats and attacks, Endpoint Detection and Response Software can be deployed, which comprises tools that are capable of intercepting security threats and protecting devices against malware, ransomware, phishing, trojans and other threats.

The COVID-19 pandemic pushed several businesses to hastily adopt remote working practices and open up their network connections to employees working from home. Among the many problems that this brought about in the overall IT infrastructure management, there were issues such as the use of remote desktop (RDP), a Microsoft tool used for accessing Windows servers, desktops and laptops. Hackers exploited vulnerabilities related to RDP, and there was a sharp upswing in such cyberattacks. According to Kaspersky, a cybersecurity company, RDP attacks went up from 969 million in 2019 to 3.3 billion in 2020 (Business Wire, 2020). Another cybersecurity company, ESET, reported that there was a 768 per cent growth in Remote Desktop Protocol (RDP) attacks during 2020 (Palmer, 2021). Other important issues related to remote working include insecure connections and the use of Shadow

IT. IT networks in office environments have strong security mechanisms and controls in place, whereas when connectivity is extended to a user's home, his network security in terms of router configurations and Wi-Fi controls is not robust in security terms, enabling hackers to sneak in. Add to it the problem of Shadow IT, which refers to applications and devices not authorised by IT departments, such as Torrents, Gmails, Dropbox, Skype, Slack, WhatsApp, Zoom, Signal and other similar software, and you have a nice cocktail of vulnerabilities available for hackers to exploit. Randori, a provider of attack surface management platforms, in its State of Attack Surface Management 2022 report, indicated that nearly 7 in 10 organisations have been compromised by Shadow IT in the past year. CISCO, the networking giant, concurs by stating that 80 per cent of company employees use Shadow IT (IBM, n.d.).

Measures to prevent network attacks—apart from basic cybersecurity measures like firewalls, intrusion detection systems, antivirus, VPNs and endpoint security systems—also involve more strategic approaches such as Zero-Trust (trust nothing, validate everything), Cloud Access Security Broker (monitors all activity and enforces security policies), Secure Access Service Edge (used to deliver wide area network and security controls as a cloud computing service) and Micro-segmentation.

Zero-day Attacks

Smart hackers are always on the lookout for new vulnerabilities that they can use to launch malicious attacks. On the other side, there are defenders who are also looking for vulnerabilities so that they can secure themselves, often with the help of vendors who have provided them with the software in the first place. Vendors, on their part, are keen to fix vulnerabilities and make their software bug-free and more secure. In all this, when a hacker finds a vulnerability that they can exploit before the software developers have found a fix for it, it is called a zero-day attack. Zero-day attacks can involve the use of various types of malware, spyware, or just unauthorised access to user information.

Given the wide usage of Microsoft Office, it is heavily targeted by hackers. In early 2017, hackers launched a series of cyberattacks using a malware called Dridex—a banker trojan. The trojan enabled hackers to embed malicious code in Microsoft Word documents, which would get triggered when opened. This zero-day attack was brought to the notice of Microsoft only in April 2017, after millions of users had already been targeted (Frankenfield, 2022).

Amid the COVID-19 pandemic, the word 'Zoom' became a household name, with most people either conducting video conferences via Zoom's video conferencing platform or attending one. Businesses around the world took to using Zoom in a big way, as it was simple and easy to use. However, there were also zero-day vulnerabilities which hackers started exploiting. In March 2020, one such vulnerability allowed hackers to share their own content (audio, video and images) by getting into public meetings (Rocket IT, 2021). This content was often inappropriate and included pornography and other undesirable material. They further planted links in chat windows, which would lead to fake websites, malware downloads and credential compromise. While this zero-day vulnerability was fixed, a new word was added to the internet lexicon called 'Zoombombings'.

Supply Chain Attacks

In recent times, supply chain attacks have gained great prominence. As organisations have taken steps to strengthen their cybersecurity arrangements, hackers have looked for easier ways to launch cyberattacks. A supply chain attack, also referred to as a value-chain or third-party attack, happens when a threat actor seeks to gain access to an organisation's systems or data via a supply chain partner, including third parties such as a vendor, contractor, service provider, or consultant. The outsourcing of various services across organisational functions, including IT services, involves providing some degree of access to organisation systems and data to improve operating efficiencies. Given the cost advantages coupled with specialist offerings that can be availed by organisations to become more competitive, the modern-day enterprise is actually an extended enterprise, which includes partners and associates across the value chain. Typically, supply chain partners include many small to medium organisations that may not have the same robust cybersecurity as larger enterprises who have greater resources at their disposal to deal with cyber threats and attacks. It is important to consider that third-party vendors that provide applications and services to an organisation also make use of components and services provided to them by others. Hence, supply chains offer a massive attack surface for hackers.

A January 2022 report published by Anchore, a software company dedicated to securing the supply chain, found that 62 per cent of organisations that they studied were targets of supply chain attacks (Anchore, 2022). Another report suggested an alarming increase of a 742 per cent average annual increase in software supply chain attacks (Plumb, 2023).

Four major supply chain attacks in recent times have made security experts and governments around the world take notice. The attacks were SolarWinds, Kaseya, Log 4J and Microsoft Exchange. For its sheer audacity and the panic that it caused, the SolarWinds attack is representative of a supply chain attack that shook the internet world like never before. The attack was a well-designed plot which could potentially have caused enormous damage in the cyber world. The attack made headlines all over the world with words like 'worst nightmare', 'hackers' masterclass', 'largest and most sophisticated hack' and 'act of recklessness' being used to describe its magnitude and advanced nature. It was an earthquake in the cyber world with a magnitude of 8!

SolarWinds is a US-based company founded over two decades ago in Tulsa, Oklahoma. It is in the business of providing software for managing networks and IT infrastructure. The company now has its headquarters in Austin, Texas, and development centres in other locations and offices around the world. Orion is one of its products that enables infrastructure monitoring and management and simplifies IT administration for different implementation models, such as on-premises, hybrid and SaaS environments, via a single interface. Like most software product companies, SolarWinds regularly provides bug fixes, security enhancements and updates to its customers.

Various reports indicate that the hackers were working on injecting malicious code in a software update, which would then enable them to get into networks of Orion's customers. At the end of 2020, at the time the SolarWinds attack was first discovered by FireEye (a cybersecurity company who were also a victim), Orion had nearly thirty-three thousand customers around the world, and among them were many Fortune 500 companies, government agencies and technology companies. First, the hackers tried out a proof of concept by modifying code in a SolarWinds update. Once this was done successfully, they held back till they were able to deliver a backdoor via an update, through which hackers could access and impersonate users and accounts of target organisations. Furthermore, the malware also enabled hackers to access system files and escape detection by blending in with normal SolarWinds activity. Such development activity would have involved great skill and also a large number of developers. According to Microsoft, such an effort would have required up to a thousand engineers (Osborne, 2023).

Sunburst was the name given to the payload containing the malicious code that was introduced in the Orion software update. The level of sophistication of the attack methodology can be gauged from the fact that the malicious code contained about 3,500 lines of encrypted code, cleverly designed to pass off in Orion's communication with other IT infrastructure as regular system communication. Later investigations revealed that the malware could remain undetected as the code had properties of 'washing its tracks'. This type of unprecedented sophistication set alarm bells ringing right up to the White House (Hernandez, 2021).

FireEye (now Madiant), an intelligence-led security company, discovered the attack in a somewhat unusual way. A member of the FireEye security team found an employee having two phones that were connected to their networks. On enquiring with the concerned employee, it was found that the second phone was not his. Weeks of further investigations revealed that there had been an intrusion, and hacking tools that were used by FireEye for their own security work were stolen. Once FireEye experts were convinced that the source of the problem was Orion, they reported the matter to the Federal Bureau of Investigation (FBI) (Hernandez, 2021).

The next step involved getting past the security checks and audits done by SolarWinds before they put their own seal of approval and shipped the update to their 33,000 customers. This stage went through successfully for the hackers, and about 18,000 customers actually installed the patch update, making themselves vulnerable to further attacks.

Attribution of a cyberattack is often a complex task, especially in a sophisticated attack such as the SolarWinds attack. Anonymity is one of the basic characteristics of the internet, giving hackers escape routes and deniability. In this case, the finger was pointed towards a highly skilled and organised group which could devote months of effort to launch such an attack. Motives are also a leading indicator of who could be behind the attack. Here, the motive of the hackers remains a mystery. While the attack could potentially have caused great damage across government agencies and large corporations, the actual damage was limited to intelligence gathering. All this suggested that this could be the handiwork of a group working on behalf of a government, such as the Russians or the Chinese, who could be fostering such groups. One thing that this supply chain attack proved was that a major global cyberattack could be launched via the technology supply chain, thereby cutting across sectors and geographies. Cozy Bear, a Russian hacker group which also goes by the name Nobelium (among other names), was eventually blamed for the attack (Osborne, 2023).

At the end of the day, the SolarWinds attack was a landmark of sorts. It showed how hackers could cause major harm across organisations, including government agencies, major corporations, defence establishments and even critical infrastructure. Reports suggest that those affected by the Solar Winds attack included the Top 10 Telecom companies, 425 Fortune 500 businesses and even parts of the Pentagon, the Centres for Disease Control and Prevention, the State Department and the Justice Department (Bhardwaj, 2022). However, this was never confirmed.

As reports about the attack circulated among the cybersecurity community, it seemed that all hell had broken loose, simply considering its ramifications and possible catastrophic implications. Cybersecurity experts in the US government and policy-making levels went into a huddle to create new policies, which were released in the form of an Executive Order on Improving the Nation's Cybersecurity by the Biden administration in May 2021. This order encourages companies—especially technology vendors of the federal government—to create what is known as a software bill of materials (SBOM). An SBOM is a list of all the external components used in the development of applications, including open-source software (The White House, 2021). This move is designed to take security measures down to the level of every third-party component and sub-component to ensure version updates, as well as fix overall responsibility for the software provided on the concerned vendors.

Based on reports from across the world, it would seem that the SolarWinds hack did not go much beyond backdooring many organisations of strategic importance and proving to the perpetrators and the world at large that such an attack could be pulled off. However, since the entire operation lasted for at least nine months, it is not impossible to visualise that the hackers could have gathered important information apart from gaining experience in launching large-scale attacks.

The other three major supply chain attacks (Kaseya, Log4J and Microsoft Exchange) are covered in a later chapter devoted to this topic.

Spycraft and Cyber Espionage

Spycraft is an old game, surveillance and eavesdropping being among its key components. Other important elements of spycraft are identifying sources of intelligence gathering, monitoring, deception, stealth, analysis and remaining undetected as long as possible. Over time, the fundamentals have not changed, but the tools and technologies have undergone transformative changes. From what was earlier heavily focused on human intelligence, we have now moved to an era of technology-based intelligence (TechInt). Edward Lucas, in an article titled 'The Spy Craft Revolution', states that "Changes in technology, politics and business are all transforming espionage. Intelligence agencies must adapt—or risk irrelevance". All things considered, the use of technology is a major driver of change, and it is those who can harness the power of technology that will have an edge (Lucas, 2019).

While governments have developed their own systems of surveillance and cyber espionage, it is hacking groups that dominate the landscape where new technologies are released everyday. Being nimble-footed and flexible, these hacker groups (and even some 'lone wolves') are quick and adept at putting them to use for malicious purposes.

Spyware is software that helps gather information about a person or organisation and sends it to another entity. The intent behind using spyware is usually malicious, but it could also be used by employers, security teams and parents to 'keep an eye' to avoid any untoward or harmful incident. Websites also may use spyware to track the online behaviour of their consumers, including their preferences, to promote the sale of products that may appeal to them. The common factor among those deploying spyware is that they want to remain undetected. Just like other forms of attacks, there are specialised technologies, tactics and procedures associated with spycraft and cyber espionage.

In the modern world, spycraft is increasingly becoming a part of statecraft. It can be directed towards not only known sovereign enemy countries but also against media, political opponents, militant groups and even common citizens. Among the early instances of state-sponsored cyber espionage that came into the limelight was an operation called Titan Rain. Starting in 2003, it was reported that Chinese hackers, using a variety of methods, performed attacks on US defence and foreign ministries, which lasted till 2007. The complicity of the Chinese government was never proven.

Technologies, Tactics & Procedures (TTPs) used in Cyberespionage

Infiltration & Hacking	**Monitoring & Tracking**	**Data Leaks/Code Breaking**
Social Engineering	Phone, Wireless tapping	Cryptographic attacks
Social Media, Phishing, Honey Trapping, Sexpionage	Geographical Information Systems (GIS)	Rubber-hose cryptanalysis
Video (CCTV/Internet Traffic), Chat and Audio surveillance	Geographical Positioning Systems (GPS)	Black-bag cryptanalysis
Forgery	Satellite Tracking	Hold back validation test
Front offices	Fibre tapping	Steganography
Identity theft, deep fakes	Internet of Things, Smart devices, Cover listening devices	Screeners
Backdoor-Hardware/ Software	Concealing objects in a book	Zero-width spaces
MAC Address Anonymization	Eavesdropping	Harvest now, decrypt later

Key changes that have led to the use of advanced technologies being deployed in recent years for cyber espionage include the introduction of smartphones and smart devices, the proliferation of social media, advancements in monitoring and tracking technologies like GPS, GIS and satellite monitoring systems, as well as the deployment of skilled and trained hackers. The SolarWinds attack is perhaps an important instance where hackers used their skills to craft and implement one of the most serious cyber espionage attacks on strategic targets in the United States by exploiting a new methodology of setting up backdoors through security updates of a key software vendor.

It is alleged that Chinese hackers have acquired specialised skills (TTPs), considering that in 2010, they launched Operation Aurora, which was aimed at over 20 international companies, including big names like Google, Yahoo and Adobe. These attacks exploited a vulnerability in Microsoft's Internet Explorer and blended stealth programming and encryption techniques. A year later, Chinese hackers were reported to have performed an operation named Night Dragon, targeting the largest European and American energy businesses, including Royal Dutch Shell and Baker Hughes. These attacks were performed using multiple techniques and technologies, such as social engineering, trojans, remote control software and other malware. The hackers successfully managed to access topographical maps and other information relating to oil reserves, making it one of the most high-profile cases of cyber espionage (Wilson, 2011).

The use of phones and social media for cyber espionage is commonplace today. The world population of smartphones is nearing the 7 billion-mark, smart devices are nearing 16 billion and social media users are nearly 5 billion in 2023. Consider the fact that there are about 25 sensors on your mobile phone and that Facebook can track over 50,000 data points about a person (Green, 2018). There is a lot of data there that can be tapped. What is more dangerous is that much of it is sensitive and can be used to cause harm.

Governments around the world have become aware and proactive when dealing with the introduction of new technologies (particularly those coming from other countries), lest it comes with built-in backdoors which can provide the manufacturers (or countries they are based in) with permanent intelligence inputs. A recent case in point is that of Huawei, a Chinese telecommunications company, which is a world leader in 5G technology and smartphones but was banned by several countries, including the United States, Australia and Japan, as they perceived the threat of cyber espionage and intellectual property theft, and hence cracked down on the Chinese technology company.

Another important but old skill used by Spymasters for centuries involves the art of deception. The means may have changed, and today, they involve the use of many tactics and procedures that are designed to deceive not only IT systems but also break in through the weakest cybersecurity element (referred to as the human factor). Hence, hacking the human behind the computer is as much an art as it is the use of science. In the words of Lt. Col Pavithran Rajan, an army intelligence veteran, "If you have to fool your enemy, you first have to fool your friends, and if you have to learn to fool your friends you have to be able to fool your family first" (ANI News, 2023).

The art of deception in cybercrime is the art of 'hacking people', using cyber techniques that rely on human weaknesses and vulnerabilities. Honey trapping is an espionage practice that involves developing romantic or intimate relationships for interpersonal, political and monetary gain or to obtain sensitive information. The advent and explosion of social media platforms have boosted the ability of hackers and cybercriminals to trap targets.

In 2017, Facebook alone conceded that up to 270 million accounts on their platform were illegitimate (The Week, 2017). This could imply that these could be either bots or honey traps. These honey trap accounts are created with carefully crafted profiles, mostly of females (though not always so). These accounts are then used for befriending people of importance in high places or in strategic sectors, such as the military, police or R&D. First, a degree of trust is built, which is then used to lure/threaten the victims to reveal sensitive information. In 2019, India identified 150 social media profiles which were being used by Pakistan to honey-trap Indian army officers into leaking state secrets. To prevent future damage, soldiers were advised to remove social media apps such as Facebook, Instagram, Tinder and dozens of others from their phones (Spyscape, 2023).

Advanced Persistent Threats (APTs)

An advanced persistent threat is a sophisticated, sustained cyberattack in which threat actors set up an undetected presence in an organisation's network with a view to meeting their objectives, including the stealing of sensitive and confidential information. APTs are different from normal cyberattacks in several ways. Firstly, the targets of these attacks are carefully chosen to meet strategic or political goals through sabotage, exfiltration, or exposure of sensitive data. Targets are often government agencies or large corporations that may be data-rich in terms of intellectual property, trade secrets, sensitive employee and customer information, as well as other confidential information that can be leveraged for future gains. Typically, these attacks are carried out by well-organised, well-resourced threat actors who may even have the backing of sovereign powers.

Secondly, APTs are not a hit-and-run operation but one where timelines can be stretched based on the progress made in terms of accomplishing the goals and objectives of the attack.

Thirdly, APT attacks often use multiple technologies and employ sophisticated techniques during various stages of the attack. The initial goal is always to establish a long-term hidden presence in a target account to be able to access and gain control over key information assets. Threat actors launching APTs use distraction techniques by initiating attacks from multiple locations to keep security teams busy while they are probing weaknesses and vulnerabilities to push their way into an account. Tools used in APT attacks are usually capable of bypassing traditional detection tools, which rely on signature-based detection techniques by using advanced techniques, such as file-less malware. Other tools are also deployed, like remote file inclusion (RFI), SQL injection and cross-site scripting (XSS), and these are often used by threat actors to 'land-and-expand' within a targeted network. The next objective is to establish persistence, which is done using trojans and backdoors. Lastly, it is important to note that APTs are complex attacks and are directed towards infiltrating and controlling an entire network over a long period of time.

Unlike a standard hit-and-run attack, a successful APT attack is carried out in multiple stages, as shown in the table below:

APT Attack Stages

Stage One	Reconnaissance, information gathering and initial infiltration. After gaining access, malware deployment in the form of installing trojans, backdoors and establishing an outbound connection to the hackers' Command and Control system is carried out.
Stage Two	Attackers aim to expand their presence across the organisational network, including gaining privileged access.
Stage Three	Undertake the exfiltration and extraction of valuable data/information assets while remaining undetected.
Stage Four	Based on the goal of the attack, at this point, the APT group may create massive damage, impairing the organisation's systems or taking over key assets such as websites or data centres.
Stage Five	Once the APT attack has met its objectives, hackers take steps to cover their tracks, remain undetected and continue their presence inside the network. After gathering more information and discovering more attack opportunities, they may launch follow-up attacks.

Tell-tale signs that an APT is in progress are the creation of new user accounts, logins being used mainly during non-working hours, the presence of trojans, which are used as a backdoor and the creation of new data bundles for exfiltration. Timelines for an APT to escalate could vary from a few hours to a few months, depending on the attacker's objectives. Other attack vectors used are remote file inclusion (RFI), SQL injections and cross-site scripting (XSS), with a view to strengthening the attackers' foothold in a targeted network.

The GhostNet attack is among the first APTs and was discovered in March 2009. Allegedly, conducted by hackers backed by the Chinese government, the target of the attack was the Tibetan community. China denied any knowledge of the attack, which was executed in a planned and sophisticated manner. Spear-phishing emails containing a payload of trojan horse malware were sent out. Once downloaded on a user system, the malware enabled the execution of commands from a remote command and control system. The stage was then set to download further malware that would enable greater control of the targeted system (Manage engine Log 360 2023).

The malware used in the attack was capable of recording audio and video and could be used to monitor the goings-on at the locations where it was installed. It was widely reported that GhostNet was targeted at over a hundred countries. Several embassies, including those of India, South Korea, Indonesia and Romania, were among the victims, as were The Asian Development Bank and ministries of foreign affairs of Bangladesh, Brunei, Indonesia, Iran, Latvia and the Philippines.

In 2016, an APT was launched against a Ukrainian power facility, Prykarpattyaoblenergo. In December, nearly seven hundred thousand people of the Ivano-Frankivsk region were left without power to face the bitter wintry conditions. The hackers deployed BlackEnergy, a deadly malware that is used to conduct DDoS attacks, cyber espionage and information destruction attacks. The hackers also deployed KillDisk, a malware that permanently deletes any data on physical disk drives without any chance of recovery (Weinberg, 2021). The hackers used a full bag of dirty tricks that included spear phishing, credential theft, remote access exploits and DoS telephony attacks. Organisations can protect themselves better by proactively implementing air-gapping between IT systems and Operations Technology (OT) systems, micro-segmenting their networks, updating their firmware and software in time and maintaining close monitoring of their network.

Cyberattacks have been continuously evolving over the past three decades. In recent times, the introduction of new technologies such as IoT, 5G and AI/ML have provided more opportunities for attacks. In the technology world, it is a proven fact that new technologies have many vulnerabilities which are discovered and fixed over a period of time. In the interim, hackers seize the moment to exploit these vulnerabilities and launch attacks. The World Economic Forum observed in its 2018 report that offensive cyber capabilities are developing more rapidly than our ability to deal with hostile incidents. At this point, the scales are tilted in favour of the hackers while defenders play the catch-up game.

There are several techniques to deploy in cyberattacks, as well as several ways to use them against individuals or establishments. It is important to note that cyberattacks can also be viewed as *Syntactic attacks*—those that involve the use of malware like viruses, worms and trojans, and *Semantic attacks*—which involve the dissemination of incorrect information to damage the credibility of target resources or to cause direct or indirect harm. Examples of Semantic attacks include defamation and slander, stock manipulation schemes, phishing, drive-by downloads, file and multimedia masquerading, domain typo squatting, advertising and other semantic social engineering attacks that aim to deceive.

Cyberattacks today are relentless, and organisations are increasingly exposed to various types of harm, including economic, reputational, cultural, political, physical and psychological harm. Cybersecurity is a fast-moving game. If you do not learn to play it well, you may have to pay the price!

4

Another One Bites the Dust: The World's Biggest Data Breaches

The most important thing in cybersecurity is not avoiding failure but recovering each time we fail. The world's biggest data breaches tell us the story of high-impact events that brought organisations across sectors to the brink, threatening their very existence and survival.

It takes years for organisations to successfully establish themselves in their sphere of activity. To become leaders in what they do means defeating their competitors with foresight, innovative products and services, differentiators and the ability to make the lives of their consumers better. However, a cyberattack or a data breach could potentially destroy an organisation's market position, reputation, and even threaten its future. Large data breaches involve not only the exposure of an organisation's own information assets but also include sensitive data that they hold (as custodians) about their customers, employees and suppliers, potentially putting all of them at risk of financial loss and other forms of cyber harassment. Larger organisations generally can weather the aftermath of a data breach and recover from it, but not without their share of losses. Smaller organisations that are less resilient could even fold up because of a cyberattack or data breach.

Today, it is not a matter of debate that mechanisms to prevent a data breach are essential. But there are other questions within such issues that still do not get their due share of management attention: What should we do if a breach does occur? What is our response and recovery strategy? How can we minimise the impact of the breach? How should we classify the incident? Who and what should we be reporting the incident to? What are the compliance issues that we need to consider? Who will communicate with different stakeholders, such as regulatory bodies, investigation agencies, employees and the media? What steps must be taken to avoid a fresh attack or data breach? How much cyber insurance do we have, and what is required to trigger the claim?

The answer to these questions must be a part of an organisation's cyber incident playbook, where every action to be taken in the event of a crisis caused by a cyberattack is documented and available to those who are responsible for each action point. Yet, when it comes to implementation, even the best and biggest of companies falter and make mistakes that only compound their losses and enhance the impact, which otherwise could have been contained to a minimum.

Technology and Social Media

The world of information technology is full of examples of companies that became massively successful on the global stage by pioneering and leveraging internet technologies to provide products and services that were quickly lapped up by millions of consumers. Yahoo! Or Yahoo Inc. was an early entrant in the business of offering online services, which included a search engine, email services, directory services, a news portal and more. It was founded in 1994 by Jerry Yang and David Filo while they were students at Stanford University in California. In the late nineties, Yahoo was locked in a battle with Google to dominate the search engine market. At the same time, Yahoo was expanding its product portfolio by releasing new products as well as through acquiring smaller companies, including Rocketmail and ClassicGames.com, which eventually became Yahoo! Mail and Yahoo! Games, as well as the photo and video-sharing platform Flickr. It also acquired a 40 per cent stake in the Chinese e-commerce giant Alibaba. In January 2000, Yahoo's shares touched an all-time high, and its market cap rose to USD 125 billion, making it the most valuable company in the world at that time. By 2012, a series of events, starting with the meltdown in internet stocks, led to a steep fall in Yahoo's market cap to USD 19 billion (Furtado, 2016). In the same year (2012), Yahoo appointed a new CEO, Merissa Mayer. Little did she know that during her tenure, the company would face what is considered the biggest data breach in history, which involved the compromise of personal information pertaining to three billion user accounts.

In the year 2013, a large number of Yahoo mail users reported that their accounts were hacked. While it was suspected that these were on the accounts of users clicking on links provided by hackers in phishing emails, Yahoo, on its part, identified some more security vulnerabilities and plugged them. The following year (2014), hackers reportedly obtained Yahoo usernames and passwords again from a third-party server and using them got more names and email IDs. Yahoo reset all passwords to halt the attackers, but the damage this time was more widespread. While Yahoo had taken some actions to contain the impact of the data breaches, they did not bring it to the attention of law enforcement agencies or the public at large.

It was only in September 2016 that Yahoo admitted that they had been hacked in 2014, and that Personal Identifiable Information (PII) of users, such as their names, email addresses, phone numbers, security questions and answers, dates of birth and encrypted passwords were compromised to the extent of 500 million accounts.

In July 2016, Yahoo received an offer of USD 4.83 billion from Verizon, the telecom giant, for a takeover. This was a delicate moment in its history for Yahoo, and any admission of a hack would have a negative impact on the takeover price and even the takeover itself.

It was only three months later, on December 14, 2016, that Yahoo announced that it had suffered its biggest-ever security breach, affecting a billion user accounts. The hack was believed to have been carried out by using forged cookies to obtain access to user accounts without using a password. A forged cookie is designed to impersonate a legitimate user without knowing their password. It enables an attacker to evade authentication mechanisms and, in some cases, can even bypass multifactor authentication.

In June 2017, Verizon completed their acquisition of Yahoo, but at the final price of USD 4.48 billion, a full USD 350 million lower than their earlier offer. The difference in price was attributed to the impact of the data breach.

In October 2017, Yahoo, in an updated assessment of the hack, stated that it now believed that all its three billion accounts at the time of the 2013 breach could have been affected. "Every Yahoo Account That Existed In Mid-2013 Was Likely Hacked", ran a headline (Selyukh, 2017). The hack is now considered the largest-ever hack of user records.

Yahoo blamed a "state-sponsored actor" for the initial cyberattack in 2014 (Kan, 2017). What is noteworthy is that the hack, which began in 2014 through a spear-phishing email, eventually led to the world's biggest data breach.

The trail of losses continued for several years. In 2019, Yahoo struck a deal with millions of people who were affected and filed lawsuits against it for USD 117.5 million. This settlement covered 194 million people (approximately 896 million accounts) and included USD 55 million for victims' out-of-pocket expenses and other miscellaneous costs, USD 24 million for credit monitoring for two years, up to USD 30 million for legal fees, and up to USD 8.5 million for other expenses (Stempel, 2019).

Yahoo, which was by this time a part of Verizon Communications Inc., had been blamed for being slow to disclose three data breaches affecting about three billion accounts from 2013 to 2016. To demonstrate its commitment to the long-term cybersecurity of Yahoo platforms, Verizon pledged to spend USD 306 million between 2019 and 2022 on information security, which was five times what Yahoo spent from 2013 to 2016. It further pledged to quadruple Yahoo's security staff (Stempel, 2019).

Four key lessons from the Yahoo data breach are: (a) to have strong preventive measures to protect user account information (the use of multi-factor authentication is an important measure in this context), (b) to create greater awareness among the user community which can help ward off phishing and other social engineering attacks, (c) to ensure timely reporting of major cyber events that could have an adverse impact on the company and other potential victims and (d) the impact of a data breach often has a long tail, which includes regulatory scrutiny, lawsuits, costs and efforts towards rebuilding security systems.

The Redmond (Washington State) headquartered Microsoft Corporation is among the big five American technology companies in the world, alongside Apple, Amazon, Alphabet (parent company of Google) and Meta Platforms (formerly Facebook). Microsoft (MS) is the world's largest software maker, providing products that range from the Windows Operating System, MS Office suite, Web browsers, Email and Cloud computing services, video games, online gaming, Xbox consoles and more. It is also a leading provider of cloud computing services, video games, computer and gaming hardware, and platforms such as Linkedin, GitHub, Skype and other online services. Given the popularity of its products and services, it is not surprising that its platforms are targeted heavily by hackers all over the world.

Microsoft is committed to providing the highest levels of security to their users, but threat actors find new ways to mount cyberattacks that enable them to get into the heart of enterprise systems and cause data breaches. In 2022 alone, Microsoft identified and blocked 70 billion emails and identity threat attacks, which represent a small part of the overall MS attack surface (Microsoft, 2023).

Timeline of Important Cyberattacks/Data Breaches—MS Products and Entities

January 2010	Using a piece of JavaScript code, hackers exploited an Internet Explorer zero-day vulnerability to breach top US companies, including Google and Adobe. The attacks went on for about three weeks. Hackers reportedly stole source code from more than 30 Silicon Valley companies targeted in the attack (Millis, 2010).

Contd.

2011–2013	Thousands of Xbox Live customers across 35 countries were lured via a phishing mail to part with their personal details, such as addresses, emails and credit card information, via a fake website. Most victims lost less than 200 pounds (GBP) from their accounts, allowing the hackers to carry on stealing money over a long period of time (Brading, 2011).
June 2012	This attack was smart in its design and sophisticated in its execution. A cyberespionage tool known as Flame was used by hackers to hijack a genuine Microsoft update to spread malware disguised as legitimate code to hundreds of computers.
May 2016	A Reuters report stated that over 250 million email usernames and passwords were discovered for sale online. These included 33 million Hotmail (owned by Microsoft) addresses as well as 40 million Yahoo addresses and 24 million Google addresses (Gilmer, 2016).
February 2018	In February 2018, GitHub survived a tsunami of web traffic from a 1.3 Terabytes per second DDoS attack. Back in 2015, GitHub was hit by a DDoS attack, which was considered the largest such attack at that time. Having learnt from this attack, GitHub in 2018 was using a DDoS protection service, which not only alerted them but mitigated the impact of the attack and limited its duration to about 20 minutes.
December 2019	A misconfigured Microsoft customer database resulted in over 250 million customer records being exposed. Surprisingly, the database was not even password-protected for over a month. Data which was compromised included the email address, IP addresses, as well as geographical and demographic data.
December 2020	Microsoft customers were caught in the crosshairs of the famous SolarWinds attack. Microsoft was one of the targeted customers, and the hackers managed to access the Microsoft users' data (Cooke, 2023).

Contd.

January to March 2021	Hackers deployed multiple zero-day exploits to attack over 30,000 organisations in the US alone (over 60,000 globally) that used on-premises versions of Microsoft Exchange Server. Hackers used these vulnerabilities to gain access to email accounts and install web shell malware, giving them ongoing administrative access to the victims' servers.
April 2021	An archive containing data from 500 million LinkedIn (owned by Microsoft) profiles was put for sale on a popular hacker forum, along with another two million records leaked as a proof-of-concept sample by the author of the post. This data breach is unique as it was an instance of large-scale data scraping. The law on data scraping is not entirely clear, though unauthorised scraping can be considered a violation under the Digital Millennium Copyright Act (DMCA) and the Computer Fraud and Abuse Act.
August 2021	Microsoft Azure, the cloud services branch of the company, suffered a data breach that gave hackers access to thousands of cloud computing files. Given that Azure has among its customers some of the world's biggest corporations, and since the cloud runs on shared infrastructure, it could have had grave consequences. Fortunately for all concerned, the hackers did not have criminal intentions and were researchers who identified a 'cross-tenant' vulnerability named 'ChaosDB', which was fixed before being maliciously exploited (Alpspach, 2022).
August 2021	Misconfiguration is a key cause of data breaches. In this instance, misconfigured settings of Microsoft Power apps caused a massive data breach consisting of the exposure of around 38 million records from over 47 companies that had stored their data on publicly accessible platforms.
August 2022	GitHub was hit by a significant software supply chain attack involving the cloning and adding of malicious code to more than 35,000 GitHub repositories. The attack affected the work of 83,000 developers from around the world.

Contd.

October 2022	It was a security research firm called SOCRadar that informed Microsoft about a misconfigured endpoint vulnerability. Data that was exposed due to this included PII such as names, email addresses, email content, company name and phone numbers, and could have included attached files pertaining to correspondence between a customer and Microsoft or an authorised Microsoft partner. BlueBleed, the name given to the data leak by SOCRadar, contained data pertaining to 65,000 entities from 111 countries and 548,000 exposed users (Cyber Kendra, 2023).

Source: https://earthweb.com/microsoft-data-breaches/

Microsoft's revenues in March 2023 have crossed USD 200 billion. It is the largest IT software vendor in the world, and its products and services are hugely popular among organisations and individuals around the world. According to the Cybersecurity and Infrastructure Security Agency (CISA), over one-third of all actively exploited vulnerabilities in 2022 are related to Microsoft systems. While there are critics of Microsoft's approach to cybersecurity, the company takes its responsibility seriously to make the cyber world a safer place.

Meta Platforms, Inc., formerly known as Facebook, Inc., is among the most valuable companies in the world. The company owns Facebook, Instagram, WhatsApp, Messenger, Quest2, Reality Labs, Mapillary, CTRL-Labs and Kustomer, among other products and services. It generates over 95 per cent of its revenue from the sale of advertising. Facebook, which has been a pioneer and leader in the growth of social media, has suffered several data breaches since its launch in 2004.

It was in June 2013 that the first instance of a major data breach took place. The personal data of over six million Facebook users was exposed due to a software bug in the contact information database collected from its 1.1 billion users worldwide, which allowed unauthorised individuals to access a user's email ID and phone number. Once they were notified of the bug, Facebook's security team fixed it within 24 hours.

2018 was a particularly bad year for Facebook as they suffered multiple data breach incidents, including the sensational story of the Cambridge Analytica scandal, which broke the plunging Facebook into a crisis. Cambridge Analytica was a British political consulting firm and a business partner of Facebook. They used Facebook data on millions of Americans without their consent or knowledge to provide analytics to the Trump presidential campaign. In all, data on 87 million users of Facebook was exposed to Cambridge Analytica, violating the privacy of these users. It was between the years of 2013 and 2015 that Cambridge Analytica exploited Facebook's Application Programming Interface (API) loophole, which they used and conducted a quiz for profile users. Facebook did not acknowledge, admit, or take any action until the media raised a ruckus in March 2018.

In effect, Cambridge Analytica broke Facebook's rules and ran a survey that would help them understand the profile and inclinations of US voters. The analytics were provided to the Trump campaign, but the jury is still out on whether the data provided swayed the election results in any way.

It was only later, in 2022, that Facebook (now Meta) agreed to pay USD 725 million (or GBP 600 million) to settle legal action over a data breach related to Cambridge Analytica, even though they did not admit to any offence (McCallum, 2022).

Facebook's woes continued through May 2018, when another software bug led to 14 million users' private posts being shared publicly even though they were at the outset posted with viewing restrictions. While the bug was fixed quickly, the posts became public without users' knowledge or consent.

Facebook faced another shocking data breach in September 2018. A simple functionality, 'View As', that enables users to view their own profile as if they were another user, was exploited by hackers to access profile data of anywhere from 50 to 90 million users. Later, in December 2018, The New York Times reported that Facebook violated user privacy by selling their data to over 150 companies (Heilingenstein, 2023).

The following year, 2019, went similarly for Facebook, with more data breaches. In March, it was discovered that up to 600 million Facebook passwords were stored in plain text, which could have potentially been exposed to Facebook employees. More shocks were in store when it was discovered that millions of Instagram passwords were also stored in plain text.

For security purposes, passwords are always stored in encrypted form so that they are not exposed to anyone. It is also important to remember that the industry's best practices for password encryption must be followed, such as bcrypt, scrypt, PBKDF2, or SHA-2.

Adobe, another well-established software company, suffered a massive data breach where usernames and passwords pertaining to 153 million records, including 3 million encrypted credit card numbers, were compromised. Since Adobe used a simple symmetric key encryption algorithm and used the same key for decryption, it was easy for hackers to crack the encryption scheme and access the passwords. Adobe reached an agreement in August 2015 to pay USD 1.2 million in legal fees, along with an undisclosed amount paid to users, to settle claims of violating the Customer Records Act and unfair business practices. It was also reported that the hackers stole Adobe's intellectual property in the form of source code of applications like Adobe Acrobat and Reader, Coldfusion and Photoshop. Each of the 38 million victims of the Adobe hack was reportedly paid USD 1.80.

Coming back to Facebook, the following month, in April 2019, 540 million Facebook user records, including account names, user IDs, comments, reactions, likes and more, were discovered on a public server. Another similar shock was in store when, in September, the personal information of 419 million Facebook users was discovered on a publicly accessible server.

Hackers have found different ways of scraping data from Facebook. In April 2021, data pertaining to over 530 million Facebook users was posted on an online hacking forum.

It was believed that the data scraping was done by exploiting a vulnerability in a utility named contact importer (Heilingenstein, 2023).

From time to time, data swathes from Twitter (another large social media company) have also turned up on online hacker forums. In May 2018, Twitter advised 330 million users to change their passwords, as they found that passwords stored were unencrypted and were accessible on their internal network.

One of the biggest security challenges faced by Twitter relates to the hijacking of accounts and impersonation of prominent personalities. In July 2020, 130 high-profile Twitter accounts were compromised by threat actors who used them to promote a Bitcoin scam. Twitter, as well as other independent media reports, indicated that the threat actors had gained access to Twitter's administrative tools, which enabled them to post tweets using the hijacked accounts. Compromised accounts included those of billionaires Elon Musk, Jeff Bezos and Bill Gates. The official Twitter accounts of Barack Obama, Joe Biden and Kanye West were also used by the perpetrators to request donations in the form of cryptocurrency (Tidy, 2020).

A series of fraudulent tweets exhorted individuals to make payments in Bitcoin to a designated account. In return, they were promised that double their money would be returned as a charitable gesture. In a matter of minutes, in response to the tweets, over 320 transactions had already taken place in Bitcoin, amounting to USD 110,000, before the tweets were removed by Twitter. Within the same month (July 2020), three people were arrested by US agencies and charged with wire fraud, money laundering, identity theft and unauthorised computer access related to the scam.

The use of encryption, multi-factor authentication and secure Application Programming Interfaces (APIs) are important developments in securing social media platforms and protecting user information.

In the future, we may enter an era where we (individuals and organisations) will become responsible for securing our own identity information. Currently, our identity is secured by the technology platforms that we subscribe to; we even make use of what is called 'federated identities', where we use our identity information stored on platforms such as Facebook or

Google to log in to other platforms. Blockchain-based Self-Sovereign and decentralised identities are being touted as the future of identity management. Self-Sovereign Identity (SSI) is a new way of managing digital identities, wherein individuals or organisations have sole ownership over the ability to control their accounts and personal data. There are no guarantees yet if this will make the digital world safer.

Healthcare

The Health Insurance Portability and Accountability Act of 1996 (HIPAA or the Kennedy-Kassebaum Act) of the US is considered a landmark in the protection of patient data. Similar legislations have now been enacted with small variations around the world by countries such as Australia, Canada, Turkey, the United Kingdom, New Zealand, the Netherlands, China and the General Data Protection Regulations (GDPR) of the European Union. Broadly classified as the protection of Personal Health Information (PHI), these regulations are designed to protect a patient's personal information like their name, address, social security number, date of birth, medical history and services provided, as well as medical and psychological conditions of patients.

The HIPAA Rules are applicable to every entity in healthcare that has access to patient records, including doctors, hospitals, insurance and other healthcare companies (called covered entities under the Act) and their business associates (who help by providing them with various types of services). Non-compliance by covered entities or their business associates could lead to fines, penalties and other liabilities.

On February 4, 2015, Anthem Inc., a leading US health insurance company, announced a massive data breach where over 37.5 million records were stolen by hackers. News of the attack sent shock waves in corporate circles, particularly in the healthcare and insurance industry.

It was in December 2014 that employees at Anthem observed suspicious database queries being made, a trend that continued for several weeks. Hackers had just grabbed sensitive data pertaining to nearly 80 million Americans, including employment information, income data, insurance policy numbers and physical addresses. While details were not made clear by the company, it was reported that hackers may have used phishing emails successfully to find their way in and get access to a large volume of personal data that was not encrypted (Sienko, 2016).

Anthem ended up with major liabilities that they had to settle, paying USD 16 million for violations of the Health Insurance Portability and Accountability Act (HIPAA) Privacy and Security Rules. Over and above this, a US District Court judge approved a USD 115 million settlement against other claims against Anthem. Adding to this, security improvement costs and the company had to incur an estimated USD 260 million overall in costs.

In 2022, the All India Institute of Medical Sciences (AIIMS), New Delhi, India's premier healthcare institute, suffered from a ransomware attack. Unconfirmed reports suggest that the data of 30 to 40 million patients could have been compromised. What was even more alarming was that the data included medical records of Very Very Important Persons (VVIPs), which could be of strategic value to hackers. The hackers made a demand of Rs 200 crores after corrupting 5 out of a total of 100 physical and virtual servers. Authorities believe that the attack originated in China. The hackers reportedly exploited vulnerabilities in a software called Zimbra, which specialises in email services (Thathoo, 2022).

Healthcare remains one of the industries that is on the hackers' radar even though there are strict regulations already in place, and compliances are mandatory. Regardless of regulatory requirements, healthcare companies, at the very least, must implement the following, given that they maintain or have access to rich repositories of patient data:

- Data encryption for sensitive data at rest and in transit
- Selective and need-based access to data
- Security policies, access controls and permissions
- User logs and behaviour monitoring

- Network traffic monitoring, reporting and audit trails
- Security training and awareness for users
- Mirrored, active data backup and disaster recovery measures

Retail and E-Commerce

Retail companies are a prime target for hackers who have a financial motive. The Verizon 2022 Data Breach Investigations Report suggests that 98 per cent of the 629 incidents in the retail sector involved a financial motive. It is, therefore, not surprising that payment systems, systems holding consumer data and user credentials are the main targets of attacks (Arctic Wolf, 2023).

The 2013 cyberattack on Target, the US retail giant, was one that created history—both for the audacious manner of its execution and the impact that resulted from it. Contact information of 70 million Target customers was compromised, in addition to payment card information pertaining to 41 million payment cards. Target, like most retailers, used Point-of-Sale (PoS) terminals to process customer payments and followed procedures as prescribed under the Payment Card Industry-Data Security Standard (PCI-DSS). It so happened that Target had given access to Fazio Mechanical Services, a contractor that provided services for their Heating, Ventilation and Air Conditioning (HVAC) systems so that they could better monitor and control the temperature, humidity and purity of the air in Target's stores.

While this by itself is not unusual, what was astounding was that the hackers got hold of a user's credentials at Fazio Mechanical through a phishing exploit. Using this, they got access to Target's network, installed malware and exfiltrated customer information over two months following their initial entry.

The fact that the hackers were able to install malware on PoS terminals across Target stores in America without being detected was an amazing feat. Payment systems that are governed by PCI-DSS standards are considered watertight in terms of security, as payment systems should be, but the hackers used their ingenuity to defeat the protection mechanisms. This occurred even though Target passed PCI compliance audits prior to the breach and had implemented security methods as required by the PCI Security Council.

The fallout of the Target cyberattack was severe. Target's CEO had to leave the company, fines worth USD 18.5 million had to be paid, and the overall cost of the breach was a whopping USD 290 million, including remediation, consulting fees and other payments (Arctic Wolf, 2023).

In 2014, an attack similar in nature to the Target attack was carried out on Home Depot, another US retail giant. A new variant of malware was used successfully by the hackers to gain access to customer data from their PoS systems. Between April and September 2014, hackers stole payment data of 52 million customers. The attack cost Home Depot nearly USD 215 million.

An important outcome of the Target incident was that payment card systems moved by 2015 to a new EMV (Europay, MasterCard and Visa) regime that was based on the Chip and Pin system, which is followed today with the aim to make the use of payment cards more secure.

In 2014, another major data breach rocked the world of retail, more precisely, e-commerce retail. The victim this time was eBay, one of the first companies to create an online consumer marketplace for goods and services. Hackers broke into eBay systems using an employee's compromised credentials and accessed up to 145 million consumer accounts. eBay admitted that the hackers copied most of the data, including email addresses, birthdates and mailing addresses. eBay further asked their users to change their passwords to avoid any further damage.

Under Armour is a pioneer, creator, marketer and distributor of branded athletic performance apparel, footwear and accessories, headquartered in Baltimore, USA. The company offers a food and nutrition application known as MyFitnessPal. In March 2018, the company suffered from a data breach that affected an estimated 150 million users of this application. Data that could have been exposed included usernames, email addresses and hashed passwords. The sheer scale and magnitude of the data breach set alarm bells rolling even as the company's share price dropped by 3.8 per cent when the news of the breach hit the markets. The company stated that passwords were protected with bcrypt, considered to be a secure hashing function, but not all passwords were similarly protected (Aiello, 2018) ().

The following is a list of common causes of data breaches (Pauli, 2015). What is apparent from this list is that even small weaknesses and security issues can lead to large-scale data breaches.

Common causes of data breaches

Weak Passwords	Application vulnerabilities	Backdoors	Lack of/weak encryption
Stolen credentials	Malware	Social Engineering	Weak administrative practices
User errors	Misconfiguration	Third-party software vulnerabilities	Poor physical security

Travel and Transportation

Travel involves sharing personal information with third parties, including travel agencies, e-commerce websites, hotels, rental car providers, airlines, insurance companies and service providers. It is implicit that the service provider will keep your personal information confidential and safe from hacking exploits and data breaches. However, in the cyber world, a cyberattack and data breach is always in the realm of possibility, regardless of the security mechanisms that the service provider has put in place. This section takes a look at three major data breaches where international corporations—Uber, British Airways and Marriott hotels—were targeted.

Uber Technologies is an American transportation conglomerate that offers a host of services to consumers around the world. They are credited with transforming urban transportation by making it convenient and cashless. In November 2016, Uber suffered a data breach. In this breach, data pertaining to 57 million employees and users, including names, addresses, phone numbers, email addresses and driver's license numbers, were compromised. Hackers used stolen credentials and got hold of an access key from a source code repository.

Uber decided not to disclose the data breach and had to pay USD 148,000 to settle a civil litigation. Furthermore, in October 2022, Joe Sullivan, the Chief Security Officer (CSO) of Uber, was convicted of a felony for his role in the coverup job (Powell, 2022).

Later, in 2022, Uber experienced another data breach. This time, it was their service provider, Teqtivity, a software company (which provides asset management and tracking service for Uber), that was the target of a cyberattack. It was reported that the data stolen included source code, IT assets, management reports, data destruction reports, Windows domain login names and email addresses and other corporate information. Furthermore, email addresses and Windows Active Directory information for over 77,000 Uber employees were also leaked. The company later said that the source code did not belong to Uber (Powell, 2022).

There are as many ways to skin a cat as there are for cybercriminals to launch malicious cyberattacks and steal data. The more data that you hold, the more attractive a target your organisation is for them. Reviewing and covering all bases regularly is the only way to minimise the damage.

Magecraft is a set of techniques from past humans that cannot be explained by science. Magecraft is also the name of hacker groups that specialise in stealing customer and payment card information through skimmers as well as other means. They have been active since 2015. Among the high-profile data breaches were Ticketmaster UK, Forbes Magazine and WordPress. However, their biggest 'hit' was British Airways (BA), the flag carrier of the United Kingdom.

All it took for the hackers was 22 lines of code that enabled them to steal the data of 380,000 customers of British Airways. Personal and financial details of passengers given at the time of booking their travel via the BA website or app were reportedly compromised. Apart from the embarrassment and loss of face caused to BA, they were fined GBP 20 million (USD 26 million) by the Information Commissioner's Office, UK, for the data breach (Ray, 2018).

Alex Cruz, the then Chairman and Chief Executive Officer, issued a public apology for the inconvenience caused to customers whose data was compromised and said that BA is committed to compensating them for any hardship they may have suffered (Read, 2018).

The Marriott Group of hotels and resorts is among the leading hotel chains in the world. In 2014, Starwood Hotels (acquired by Marriott Group in 2016) suffered a major data breach for the first time. Hackers were able to gain access to about 340 million guest records worldwide. The hackers copied and encrypted guest information, including names, addresses, telephone numbers, date of birth, gender, email addresses, passport numbers, Starwood's rewards information (including points and balance), arrival and departure information, reservation dates and their communication preferences. The attack was a source of deep embarrassment for the hotel chain, apart from facing fines and penalties. For the hackers, it resulted in a big bonanza—a database of important people that could be exploited!

Remarkably, this incident was not detected by Marriott's IT or security teams until September 2018. Inevitably, they were fined GBP 14.4 million (USD 24 million) by the UK's Information Commissioner's Office. The top priority of any hotel's IT or security team must be to encrypt guest data and set up alerts if there is any indication of a potential security breach (Whittaker, 2018). More trouble followed when, in January 2020, Marriott was hacked again in another incident that affected around 5.2 million guests. Yet again, in June 2022, Marriott suffered a data breach for the third time in four years. In this incident, credit card data and internal documents pertaining to company operations were compromised. Enhancing employee awareness through cybersecurity training, encryption of all sensitive data and adoption of new approaches like zero-trust can go a long way in preventing more such attacks.

Phishing and social engineering is the most common first step taken by hackers looking to pull off a large data breach. While there are several innovative ways in which hackers conduct phishing campaigns, here are ten ways to stop them from being successful.

Ten ways to protect yourself from phishing attacks

- Train employees to identify phishing attacks.
- Implement multi-factor authentication and encourage the use of strong passwords.
- Encourage employees to disclose the bare minimum of personal information on social media.
- Get employees to exercise care before they click on any link or open an attachment. If suspicious, they must report it to the IT team.
- Block pop-ups.
- Enable firewalls and antivirus.
- Use Virtual Private Networks (VPN).
- As far as possible, avoid visiting insecure sites (http). Secure sites (https) display a padlock.
- Install security updates on priority.
- Look out for scams and schemes that sound too good to be true or those that call for urgent action.

In too many cases, simple prevention measures could have helped avoid major cyberattacks and data breaches. Cybersecurity is a team game. It is not just IT and security teams who can ensure an organisation is safe from cyberattacks. Every employee must contribute to making security systems more robust by actively understanding and implementing security requirements.

Government and Public Utilities

Aadhar is the name of India's unique identification project under which the country's citizens have been given a unique identification number that forms the basis for accessing various government schemes and other services like banking, telecom, etc. The unique identification number is issued after capturing demographic and biometric information and works seamlessly to authenticate the identity of a person. The Aadhar project is the biggest of its kind in the world. As of November 2022, according to the Economic Survey conducted by the government, 135.2 crore Aadhaar numbers have been issued so far, almost covering India's total population. The Aadhar initiative has been hugely successful, and it's a matter of great pride for the government that 318 central schemes and over 720 state Direct Benefit Transfer schemes use Aadhaar for the targeted delivery of financial services, subsidies and benefits to citizens (Money Control, 2023).

According to the World Economic Forum's Global Risks Report 2019, the largest-ever data breach (which was actually a series of breaches) happened when records pertaining to over a billion Indian citizens were compromised. Reports in January 2018 suggested that this data was made available by cybercriminals who were charging Rs 500 for 10 minutes of access. There were several individual data breaches that constituted the 1.1 billion records which were reportedly compromised.

In 2017 and 2018, multiple data tranches were leaked through various government agencies' portals. A big incident happened in March 2018. A flaw in a software patch allowed users elevated access levels and enabled them to evade security features such as iris scan and GPS location verification. It was reported that at this time, the Aadhar database contained 1.2 billion records, although it is not known how many records were compromised. In February 2019, a misconfigured website of the government company Indane, an LPG distributor, had its customer information exposed due to the lack of an authentication mechanism on its dealer portal.

The Unique Identification Authority of India (UIDAI) in February 2019, in an affidavit in the Delhi High Court, denied that Aadhar data could have been compromised as the UIDAI uses the strongest level of encryption technology (2048-bit encryption) which is impossible to decrypt (IANS, 2019).

In neighbouring China, in 2022, a large tranche of personally identifiable information (23 Tera Bytes) was made available for sale on an underground marketplace by a hacker(s) whose identity was not disclosed.

Data related to about one billion people from China was stolen from a Shanghai police database. The dataset included names, addresses, birthdates, telephone numbers, national IDs, as well as criminal records of both Chinese citizens and foreigners who visited Shanghai. The reason for the massive data leak was a dashboard that was left exposed to the internet without a password for over a year. The sheer scale of exposure of PII makes the Shanghai Police leak top the charts in the largest-ever data breaches (Vijayan, 2022).

Energias de Portugal (EDP) is a Portuguese electric utilities company created in 1976 through the merger of 14 nationalised electricity companies. It is headquartered in Lisbon and is among the largest energy suppliers in Europe. In April 2020, the company suffered a ransomware attack. The hackers used compromised employee credentials to find their way into EDP's network. After encrypting the dataset of 10 Terabytes, the hackers exfiltrated the data, which included sensitive customer information and employee credentials. Implementation of multi-factor authentication could have saved EDP from such an attack, as even if they got hold of some employee credentials, they would have faced a block at the next stage of authentication.

In one of the most horrifying data breaches, the Office of Personnel Management (OPM) of the US government was hacked in 2015. The OPM serves as the chief human resources agency and personnel policy manager for the US Government. One of its activities is to carry out background checks as a part of the recruitment process. The hackers managed to steal PHI, PII and the financial history of over 21 million people (Parker, n.d.).

Just as major corporations are regularly targeted by hackers, so are government departments and agencies. Often, the perpetrators of cyberattacks on government and public utilities are organised hacker groups who either work in their own interest or on behalf of enemy countries. What hackers do know well is that all government systems are not equally well protected; employee weaknesses and security loopholes abound, and the payoff from a successful data breach can be huge.

Banking and Financial Services

Banking and financial services companies have historically been the most attractive target for hackers. Organisations in this industry are data-rich and can provide quick yields if hacks are successful. Apart from PII, hackers can access financial information, initiate fraudulent financial transactions and profit from the same. It is true that since banking and financial services companies either operate payment systems or hold information related to them, they have higher levels of security, making the task of causing a data breach more difficult.

The First American Financial Corporation is a financial services company that offers title insurance and settlement services to the real estate and mortgage industries. A common website design error led to the compromise of data related to 885 million credit card applications. A webpage link which led to sensitive information was not protected through an authentication mechanism required to verify user access. Poor code review practices, coupled with no monitoring of data leaks, were two major reasons for the data leak.

Equifax is a consumer credit reporting agency headquartered in Atlanta, Georgia. It is one of the three largest consumer credit reporting companies in the world. The Equifax data breach was a disaster of epic proportions, where information pertaining to more than half the American population was compromised

The Equifax scenario involved an Apache Struts vulnerability that remained unpatched for several months. Hackers used this vulnerability to gain entry to the Equifax network. The Equifax network was not segmented well enough to prevent hackers from moving across systems after gaining access. The hackers used usernames and passwords, which they found stored in plain text, to escalate privileges, which gave them deeper access.

Hackers were also able to exfiltrate data without being detected for months.

In the backlash after the data breach, Richard Smith, the CEO and Chairman of the Board of Equifax, had to step down. Personal data pertaining to 143 Americans was stolen, and the resultant crisis can well be imagined. A patch for the Apache Struts vulnerability was available in March 2017, but it was after a full two months that the patch was updated on Equifax systems. It is extremely important to install updates immediately when available, more so when they are related to security vulnerabilities. Organisations need to have clear-cut responsibilities and timelines defined to carry out these updates, or else, as it happened in this case, because of the fault of an IT engineer, the CEO of a large multinational corporation lost his job. Furthermore, the company was fined USD 700 million for the breach and overall faced an estimated USD 1.38 billion in terms of the costs related to the data breach. If all this was not enough to bring the company to its knees, there were several lawsuits and even news of Equifax executives selling company stock, violating insider trading regulations.

If only Equifax had a process to install updates in a timely manner, if only they had segmented their IT network better, if only they had monitored the data being exfiltrated—the worst data breach in history could have been avoided.

Heartland Payment Systems, Inc. (HPS) is a payment processing and technology provider based in New Jersey, USA. Founded in 1997, Heartland Payment Systems' last headquarters were in Princeton, New Jersey. In January 2008, hackers conducted an SQL injection attack on the company, whereby they injected malicious code through a web form on HPS's website. Having done this, they installed sniffer software, which they used to intercept credit card and debit card data while in transit. In all, data related to 130 million credit and debit cards was compromised.

Albert Gonzalez is an American hacker who also worked as a police informer. He was born in 1981 and, along with two other associates, was accused of stealing data from HPS. He was later indicted and was given a 20-year prison sentence.

Performing a major data breach and then bragging about it on social media sounds unreal. Yet it happened in the case of Capital One, an American company focused on credit cards, auto loans, banking and savings accounts. In 2019, an ex-employee of Amazon Web Services (AWS), Paige A. Thompson, unlawfully accessed one of the AWS servers which contained Capital One's data and stole 100 million credit card applications.

In what was one of the largest breaches that can be attributed to an 'insider', The Capital One breach was unusual in many ways. Paige Thompson can be considered an insider as she was working for Amazon, which was the designated cloud services provider for Capital One. Paige not only bragged about the breach on social media but also informed the company about the stolen data dump. It did not take long for FBI officials to figure out that she was behind the data breach. Important lessons from the Capital One data breach include security practices related to cloud platforms, as well as enhanced focus on insider threats.

Manufacturing

In most large data breaches, we have seen that datasets targeted by hackers include personally identifiable information, healthcare data, financial information, payment transactions, etc. However, there are other types of information, such as Intellectual Property, which is of great value to threat actors. In 2007, Gary Min, a research chemist working at Dupont (the chemicals major), admitted to downloading 22,000 abstracts from the company's data repository and accessed 16,706 documents that were not related to his area of work. Min, another insider, was handed an 18-month prison sentence, a fine of USD 30,000, and also a restitution order for USD 14,500. The sequence of events may not be suggestive of a major data breach until you consider that the estimated value of the technology accessed was in the range of USD 400 million.

In 2017, the NotPetya malware was creating havoc around the world. Mondelez, the food and beverage company famous for its chocolates, suffered a disastrous attack wherein 1,700 servers and 24,000 laptops were permanently damaged. In addition, Mondelez also reported the theft of thousands of user credentials. It also disrupted operations as Mondelez had difficulties in executing customer orders. Further, it impacted production facilities around the globe. Mondelez were hoping that their insurance policy with Zurich Insurance would cover its losses. To their surprise, the insurance company turned down their USD 100 million claim, saying that NotPetya was not a normal cyberattack but an act of war. Big international firms like FedEx, Merck and Maersk also suffered NotPetya attacks. The estimated losses caused by NotPetya were put at USD 10 billion on a worldwide basis (Martin, 2022).

Key takeaways that emerge from the world's largest data breaches are:

I. The growing importance of implementing strong cybersecurity measures, including technology, people and processes.

II. Most of the big data breaches were not the outcome of sophisticated methods and means. Simple security vulnerabilities and mistakes can cause large breaches.

III. Hackers are now adept at identifying targets, finding vulnerabilities and performing devastating attacks.

IV. Compliance with regulations, timely reporting and disclosure is necessary.

V. Timely breach detection and response are key to minimising damage.

VI. Insurance is not enough to cover the costs of a cyberattack or data breach. Read the fine print in insurance policies very carefully.

VII. Organisation-wide awareness of phishing and social engineering risks. Insiders can be an important threat factor and must be considered while designing security.

VIII. All security tasks must get priority (such as timely application of patches).

IX. Strong passwords, use of multi-factor authentication and encrypting sensitive data can avoid major data breaches.

X. After a data breach and the initial recovery, there is a long tail of activities, actions and costs that follow.

5

Most Bizarre Cyberattacks

There are many who would say that any cyberattack is an extraordinary event. However, there is a category of cyberattacks which is super extraordinary and can be described as weird, absurd, or bizarre. Hackers can be innovative and can go to any lengths to achieve their goals. Bizarre cyberattacks showcase the innovative ways of the hacker.

Sometimes, to break into a network, hackers must go beyond their standard bag of tricks. They need to find clever and innovative ways of defeating or bypassing security systems or luring unsuspecting users to provide them with their credentials. Hackers are also persistent in their efforts and can adapt to their target IT environment. There are occasions when their methods are ingenious and incredible, as is the case where hackers stole data from a casino through a fish tank. Truly Bizarre!

The Fish Tank Hacking

Casinos are a big business in North America. In 2017, Darktrace, a global leader in cybersecurity, announced that an unnamed casino from North America was hacked and that they had been called in to monitor some suspicious activity that was going on. Their findings, to say the least, were astounding.

The casino had installed an aquarium on its premises, which was equipped with an advanced thermostat that contained Internet of Things (IoT) sensors that were connected to and controlled via a personal computer. The objective here was to regulate the temperature of the water, monitor the fish feed, salinity and cleanliness of the tank.

An unidentified hacker gained access to the fish tank, and through this, managed to get into the casino's IT network by identifying some vulnerabilities. Ten gigabytes of data (the casino's high-roller database) was exfiltrated to a server in Finland before things were brought under control.

Smart technology is great to have, and we are more dependent on it than ever before. However, any device that is smart is also vulnerable.

The Gas Station Hacking

Everyone likes the idea of getting gas for free at a gas station. A bunch of hackers found a way to do this. Hackers used a special remote which they bought online. Through the remote, they discovered that they could crack a particular model of gas pumps installed at Total (a French Oil and Gas company) gas stations. This was made easy by lazy pump managers not changing the default password setting for the lock code, which was '0000'. Once the hackers discovered this, they were able to reset fuel prices and remove any fill-up limits.

The hackers quickly set up a smart operation wherein one of the hackers would remotely unlock the gas pump while another in a vehicle with a large tank would fill up nearly 750 gallons each time. If this was not crazy enough, they sold the stolen gas at discount pricing by advertising on social media. In all, the gang of five stole almost 25,000 gallons of gas and made around USD 170,000 before they were caught in 2019 (Cimpanu, 2019).

The Voice Spoofing Mishap

Hackers love to play with different technologies that can help them succeed in their malicious ventures. In March 2019, hackers used artificial intelligence-based (AI) software to clone the voice of a German energy company's CEO. Using voice-spoofing (voice impersonation) software, they spoofed the voice of the CEO and made a demand to the CEO of the UK subsidiary of the German energy company to transfer a sum of USD 243,000 to the account of a Hungarian supplier. All this while, the CEO of the UK firm was under the impression that he was speaking to his German boss, who gave him a deadline of one hour to complete the transaction (Stupp, 2019).

How many of us have such a high degree of situational awareness while responding to our boss or someone in authority to suspect or question them further? Cyberattacks are not just about malware, phishing and social engineering; there are elements of innovation, cunning and human psychology involved in their planning and execution.

The transfer of money was duly made, and the hackers called to say that the parent company in Germany had reimbursed the money sent by the UK firm. Then they made another call (impersonating the German CEO), asking for a second payment. As the reimbursement had not arrived and the call just received was from an Austrian number, it aroused some suspicion. Fortunately for the company, the second payment was never made.

Experts predict that the use of AI can have a major impact and help hackers automate cyberattack incidents. Going beyond voice spoofing, we now have the security challenge of dealing with deep fakes in the form of synthetic videos. Hackers can now conduct different types of scams using AI, which can lead to many problematic scenarios for the victims as well as investigators and law enforcement agencies. Cybercriminals could even use publicly available voice recordings and videos to impersonate celebrities or executives. These types of attacks will only get more sophisticated, given that the technology is available and will lead to scenarios ranging from the outrageous to the bizarre!

Rock and Roll Cyberattack

If you are a rock fan, this one is for you. In 2010, a virus, allegedly developed by the American and Israeli governments, took control of the centrifuges operating in an Iran nuclear facility, causing thousands of them to break down. The attack, more famously known as the Stuxnet attack, had a strange twist to it. The coders were not just happy to damage Iran's nuclear facilities; they were out to have some fun, too. They hijacked the workstations at the facility and used them to play

Thunderstruck, a popular rock number from the band AC/DC (McCormick, 2014).

They also uploaded AC/DC's track 'Thunderstruck' to the public address system. So, here was a cyberattack happening in the middle of the night at a nuclear facility, with Thunderstruck being played at full blast at random intervals. Absolutely weird!

Hackers Outmanouvered by Radiohead

Hackers were trumped by the victims in another strange case involving a rock band, Radiohead, a popular English rock band comprising five members: Thom Yorke, brothers Jonny Greenwood and Colin Greenwood, Ed O'Brien and Philip Selway, who faced an unusual situation. A hacker stole a mini disk archive from Thom Yorke, which had 18 hours of recordings. The hacker demanded a sum of USD 150,000 to return the stolen recordings, and if not paid, would release them to the public. The band members were in a dilemma, and after much discussion between them, they decided to release 18 hours of their recordings on Bandcamp in aid of Extinction Rebellion, a climate change group, much to the surprise of the hacker (Whittaker, 2019).

Hacking the Hacker!

Hitting back at the hacker(s) can be fun. In 2019, German programmer Tobias Fromel became a victim of a ransomware attack. He paid the hacker a sum of 670 euros but went on to hack the Muhstik malware used by the hacker. He got his revenge by extracting from the command-and-control server of the hacker hardware identities and generating unique decryption keys for 2,858 victims. Amazing case of hacking the hacker (Segun, 2019)!

Hacked Hotel

Not being able to open the door of your hotel room can be a nightmarish experience. Guests who were enjoying their stay at the Romantik Seehotel Jaegerwirt in the Austrian village of Turracherhohe were in for a rude shock when they could not open their hotel room doors. Hackers had managed to break into the hotel's systems, remotely locked the doors, and demanded a ransom. The hotel thought it best to pay the ransom to avoid inconveniencing their guests.

Of the various things you may be worrying about these days, getting locked out of your lovely hotel room in scenic Austria is probably not very high on the list. In the end, the hotel ended up having to pay about USD 1,800 (two Bitcoin) to hackers who had penetrated their systems and managed to remotely lock the hotel room doors.

Ransomware can put people into scary, life-threatening situations. Imagine getting locked in your car and not being able to get out on a cold winter's day, or hackers taking control of a hospital's systems where there are patients under intensive care. The Hollywood Presbyterian Medical Centre had to shell out a USD 17,000 ransom in Bitcoin to a hacker who seized control of the hospital's computer systems. The malware locked systems by encrypting files, and the quickest way of restoring the systems and services was to pay the fine.

Cyberattacks With Confusing Motives

An unusual cyberattack happened when all devices connected to an American university's computer network suddenly started searching for different kinds of seafood. As crazy as it sounds, hackers used IoT malware to trigger over 5,000 internet-connected devices into searching for seafood in neighbourhood restaurants. The impact of the attack (a DDoS attack) was such that it shut down the entire network after initially slowing it down. The internet-connected devices included vending machines, lamp posts, access control systems and VoIP services (Goud, n.d.). What was indeed weird was that all the IoT devices (more than 5,000 in all) started searching for seafood in nearby restaurants all at the same time. Incredible, is it not?

It was nearing midnight on a Friday in the city of Dallas, USA, when all 156 of the city's emergency alarm systems went off. The alarms were designed to warn citizens of tornadoes, storms and other extreme weather events (Smith, 2017). Citizens scrambled out of their beds in a panic as noise levels reached high decibels with the alarms blaring. There was a surge of calls to 911 and other emergency services.

The Dallas Office of Emergency Management responded to the sirens and discovered that the ringing alarms were turned on by a hacker. No major damage done here, just some hacker who perhaps wanted to show off!

Hacking for Social Justice

It is an unusual occurrence when something bad can end up with some good. Threat actors are people who are ready to cause harm in any number of ways, but here was a case where hackers using ransomware demanded that victims must donate to charity or perform acts of charity to regain access to their IT systems and IT assets instead of making payments to them. Goodwill ransomware thus forces victims to donate to the poor and patients in need. The hacker group is running a Robin Hood-esque operation. On the one hand, they are hacking innocent victims, and on the other, they are serving the poor and the sick.

Goodwill ransomware was identified in March 2022. Threat actors using it are more interested in promoting social justice rather than conventional financial reasons. Demands made by the hackers involve performing the following actions to get access to your data, photos, videos and other files that are encrypted:

1. Donate new clothes to the homeless, record the action, and post it on social media.
2. After completing the above, pick any five children below the age of thirteen and treat them to the food that they like at Domino's, Pizza Hut or KFC.
3. Go near a hospital. Identify people who may need money for treatment. Give them the money, take selfies, and post them on social media.

Does this sound like a cold-blooded bunch of hackers? Seems like there are some good ones, too.

Hacking for Jobs

Jobs with globally famous institutions, like the Marriott group of hotels, are coveted ones. Instead of going through the usual application route, a hacker used the techniques that he knew best. He conducted a phishing campaign and sent infected emails to a large number of employees of Marriott Hotels. He then gained access and stole confidential and financial information that he thought he could use to blackmail them into giving him a job. Marriotts took the help of US law enforcement agencies to lay a trap for him. A Marriott HR person (actually a secret service agent) performed a sting operation on the hacker under the pretext of an interview. The hacker, Attila Nemeth, 26, a Hungarian citizen, was arrested soon after and sentenced to 30 months in prison!

A job at Harvard University that never was. A prominent Indian news anchor and accomplished TV journalist, Nidhi Razdan, was for several months led to believe that she had a job offer to become an associate professor at Harvard. Unfortunately for her, the whole episode turned out to be a hoax. In June 2020, Razdan announced that she was leaving her job at the news channel where she had worked for 21 years to take up a teaching assignment at Harvard.

The entire process Razdan was subjected to as part of her recruitment was a charade. It was through an online search that she believed that there was a journalism faculty position available at the University's Extension School, which had a record of hiring working journalists in the past. She went ahead and submitted her resume and attended a 90-minute online interview, following which she received an offer letter on the letterhead of the University, which looked genuine.

As she prepared to go to the University by resigning from her job and initiating her visa process, she received a communication that due to the impact of COVID-19, classes were delayed till January 2021. She did not get her salary as per terms and wrote to the office of the Dean of the Graduate School of Arts and Sciences, and was shocked when they said that they had no records of her appointment (Pundir, n.d.). Clearly, someone had played a bad joke on her.

Outer Space Scams

A Japanese woman faced an outrageous situation of being scammed by a person she thought was an astronaut. The fake astronaut befriended her on Instagram and convinced her that he was a real astronaut by posting his photographs and dropping names of the US space agency, NASA, and JAXA, the Japanese space agency. Having won her trust and perhaps her love, he made an unusual request to her, asking for about USD 30,000 to hitch a ride back to Earth as he was stuck at the International Space Station. Taken in by his plight, the elderly Japanese woman sent him five payments, after which she realised that she was being conned.

A similar scam was orchestrated in 2016, when a man who claimed to be Nigeria's first astronaut put out a request for USD 3 million, saying that he was detained on a Soviet spacecraft (Al-Sibai, 2022). When it comes to cyber scams, even the sky is not the limit!

Fake Cricket Tournament

Here is the story of a fake cricket tournament conducted using all the technology at their disposal, including online betting, that truly goes from the sublime to the ridiculous. A small village was the stage where the cricket grounds (complete with boundaries and halogen lamps) for this fake cricket gambling operation were created. The promoters of the cricket tournament employed farmers, labourers and unemployed youth as players, downloaded crowd-noise sound effects from the internet, and employed a speaker who could impersonate a popular cricket commentator to make the goings-on appear authentic during the live streaming of these fake cricket matches. Using high-resolution cameras, they broadcast these fake matches on YouTube and invited bets. The operation was proceeding smoothly and hit 47 videos and 49k views on its YouTube channel (the tournament had reached the quarterfinal stage) before law enforcement agencies broke up the fake cricket league (Agence, 2022).

Fast Food Feud

McDonald's and Burger King are among the top fast-food restaurants around the world. However, they have a business rivalry going back decades, though it is true that McDonald's is almost four times the size of Burger King in terms of revenue. Back in 2013, a hacker gained control of Burger King's Twitter account and made an announcement that Burger King had been sold to McDonald's. He also changed the display name and icon to a picture of McDonald's. "We just got sold to McDonald's! Look for McDonald's in a hood near you", one post read. The hacker's mischief did not last long, as, after an hour or so, Twitter suspended the account. In the process, Burger King gained 60,000 new followers (BBC, 2013a, 2013b).

The Ashley Madison Hack

Ashley Madison is a dating website whose slogan is "Life is short. Have an affair." Their services are designed to be a discreet way for cheating spouses to date and indulge in affairs. In 2015, Ashley Madison faced a massive data breach where 300 Gigabytes of user data, which included names, banking information and private sexual information, was stolen. The hackers named Impact Team said that the website did not have even the basic security, making it easy for them to steal the data. The company paid USD 11.2 million to settle lawsuits and another USD 1.66 million in fines (Verge, 2017). The hackers leaked the data on the dark web, exposing the users of the website to a life of misery and retribution from their spouses should they find out.

Iceman, The Hacker

Max Ray Butler, aka Iceman, was a hacker who created history by stealing the credit card information of over two million people during his active hacking career. The most unusual thing about his exploits was that he not only stole information from banks, businesses and individuals but also from hackers. Max is now serving a 13-year sentence (BusinessInsider, n.d.). In the cyber world, no one is secure, including hackers themselves!

With $265 million at Stake, a Man Forgets His Password to a Bitcoin Treasure

Stefan Thomas a cryptocurrency expert who was the chief technology officer at Ripple was once paid 7002 Bitcoins for a piece of work that he did several years ago. Thomas stored all his Bitcoins in a digital wallet on a USB drive and lost the password. Over the past decade, the value of each Bitcoin has risen steeply from just a few dollars to USD 38,000. His Bitcoins are now worth around USD 265 million. The tragedy is that he needs the password. The IronKey USB drive is military grade and allows a maximum of password 10 attempts to guess the password and Thomas has already used up 8 of them. Only two attempts are remaining for Thomas to access his fortune. If he fails, the contents on the USB drive will be permanently erased.

6

Held to Ransom: Major Extortion Attacks

A ransomware attack is not just financial extortion but a means to force a targeted individual or organisation to take actions that could put at risk and jeopardise the individual concerned, the organisation, or have greater consequences that could even transcend industry or geographic boundaries.

Ransomware attacks are possibly the most feared form of attack. Quite suddenly, you lose access to your own data (Shock 1), you are faced with a demand to pay a ransom, maybe even in bitcoins in order to get your access back (Shock 2), then attackers confirm that they have exfiltrated your confidential and sensitive data to their own servers and issue a threat that it will be exposed on the internet if the ransom is not paid within a stipulated time period (Shock 3), and your IT team says that you don't have a back up to resume operations, while you can negotiate with the attackers (Shock 4). Further shocks can also be in store for you when the attackers, after receiving payment, do not give you the decryption key, demand further payment or actions, or the decryption key provided does not work, or your hardware is permanently damaged and needs to be replaced.

With all your business-critical systems rendered inaccessible and work disrupted in such a way that your customers have started to suffer the impact of your ransomware attack, you are as helpless as you can ever be.

Ransomware attacks are considered a serious national security risk around the world. Different types of institutions, from small to large business enterprises, colleges, hospitals, schools, municipal corporations and other institutions, have been victims of ransomware attacks. One in every five cybercrimes in 2022 was a ransomware attack. It is also no surprise that the use of phishing is the most popular entry strategy for hackers (Griffiths, 2023b).

A ransomware attack is a grave crime, but threat actors perform these attacks with great impunity without the fear of being brought to book. The anonymity that the internet offers, along with weak law enforcement mechanisms, which are mostly ineffective in dealing with this type of cross-border crime, provide a favourable environment for threat actors to operate.

Even amateur hackers today can launch ransomware attacks as the tools of the trade are easily available and do not call for a great degree of expertise or high investment from them. Ransomware as a Service (RaaS) enables hackers to hire ransomware software along with execution manuals and even pay through profit-sharing models.

In recent years, ransomware attacks have been on the increase and in 2021 alone, there were over 620 million ransomware attacks. Some of the major hacker groups engaged in ransomware attacks around the world are LockBit, REvil, BlackCat and Black Basta.

Attack on the Costa Rica Government

Here is the story of a ransomware attack that became a national emergency. On 10 May 2022, Rodrigo Chaves, the President of Costa Rica, declared a national emergency as the country faced a major ransomware attack. The attack disrupted several government services and also customs and tax platforms. In all, nearly thirty institutions of the government were affected. Other major institutions impacted included the Ministry of Finance, the Ministry of Science, Innovation, Technology and Telecommunications (MICITT), the National Meteorological Institute, state internet service provider RACSA, the Costa Rican Social Security Fund, the Ministry of Labor and Social Security, the Fund for Social Development and Family Allowances and the Administrative Board of the Municipal Electricity Service of Cartago. The private sector was also hit by the ransomware attack, and several firms were forced to operate manually.

A ransom demand of USD 10 million was made by a Conti group in exchange for not exposing the information stolen from the Ministry of Finance. This data might have contained sensitive information, such as tax returns of individuals and companies operating in Costa Rica.

On May 16, President Chaves announced that the country was in a state of war against a terrorist group that was threatening to overthrow his government and was being aided in their efforts by the Conti Group. In the President's own words, he described the situation as follows (Mora Por Andrea, 2022):

> We do not know; we do not have information about who is paying us taxes correctly and incorrectly. There is a huge impact on the international trade process since the Customs TICA system is not working. We do not know how the country's budget execution is progressing: Costa Rica does not know how much of the budget each person is spending, whether we are going to pay ourselves or not. We are paying salaries almost blindly based on previous payrolls, which represents a huge challenge for the future. What happens if someone is paid more than is due and we are repeating the same payroll? There are people who are being paid less by the State than they should be for using old forms. This represents a huge risk because the systems are not flexible to recover excess payments. We have 27 institutions attacked and 9 institutions very affected, including the Ministry of Finance, which is the one that receives the income and makes the expenses of the State. They want to drown us through the financial system of the State's public finances.
>
> – Rodrigo Chaves Robles, President of Costa Rica

On May 31, 2022, another group called the Hive Ransomware Group carried out an attack against the Costa Rican Social Security Fund.

Ransomware attacks are network-based. Any devices connected to the internet can be targeted via phishing emails, as it happened in this case. According to the Director of Digital Governance, Jorge Mora, investigations revealed that the attack started in April. In all, they found about 35,000 malware communication requests, 10,000 phishing incidents and 60,000 attempts to take remote control of IT systems. In addition to this, there were 60,000 attempts to mine cryptocurrencies using the computing infrastructure of nearly 100 state institutions (Grosser, 2022).

The next stage in the sequence of events was that after successful entry, the malware starts to encrypt key files on the victim's systems and/or lock the screens.

The Costa Rican government did not pay the initial ransom. The ransomware group, as of 9th May 2022, leaked most of the 600 gigabytes of data that they had encrypted.

According to FBI estimates, Conti ransomware accounts for over a thousand ransomware attacks, with payouts exceeding USD 150 million, making it the most dangerous and damaging ransomware ever. The US Department of State announced a bounty of USD 15 million for the arrest of those groups that deployed Conti (Crothers, 2022).

Meanwhile, losses related to the Costa Rica ransomware attack were estimated to be USD 30 million for every single day that the government could not operate normally. This was a unique case of a nation's critical systems completely rendered unusable by a ransomware attack.

Swissport Ransomware Attack

Swissport International Ltd. is an aviation services company with its headquarters in Zurich, Switzerland. It provides airport ground handling, lounge hospitality, maintenance, cleaning and cargo-handling services. The company has 66,000 employees and handles nearly 300 million passengers and around 5 million tons of cargo annually. Swissport operates in 50 countries and over 300 airports around the world.

A tweet by Swissport posted at 2.50 PM on 4th February 2022 said that "A part of Swissport IT infrastructure was subject to a ransomware attack". The Tweet further added that the attack had largely been contained. Other reports indicated that the cyberattack happened at 6 AM on the previous day and caused minor delays for 22 flights. The bad news was yet to be broken (Toulas, 2022).

The BlackCat ransomware group, aka ALPHV, is among the most sophisticated ransomware operators in the world. They not only claimed responsibility for the attack but also said that they had 1.6 terabytes of sensitive data that they wanted to sell. The data that they had stolen included the names of passengers, their nationality, passport numbers, religion, email IDs, phone numbers, etc.

The service providers Swissport are part of the critical infrastructure of several countries as they operate airports across the world. The passenger and cargo data that they are holding are invaluable from a hacker's viewpoint. Cyberattacks on critical infrastructure can be devastating. Just a few days before the Swissport attack, there was a series of attacks across Europe, including an attack against Oiltanking, a German fuel distribution company's major oil terminals in Belgium and multiple European seaports (Henriquez, 2022).

According to BleepingComputer, a website that covers technology news, BlackCat has been operating in several countries, including the USA, Australia and India. Their ransom demand is generally in the range of USD 400,000 to USD 3 million, payable in Bitcoin or Monero. Victims who opt to pay in Bitcoin must pay an additional fee of 15 per cent over the demanded ransom. To keep the pressure on victims to pay, BlackCat uses additional cyber threats like running a DDoS attack until they pay a ransom. Looking at all aspects of the Swissport ransomware attack, it is one the most sophisticated attacks of its kind (Sharma, 2022). Overall, this is a highly erudite ransomware operation, with the threat actors clearly considering all aspects of the attack.

Types of Ransomware

WannaCry	Ryuk	Petya
Revil	Locky	CryptoWall
Conti	Darkside	TeslaCrypt
Scareware	CTB-Locker	Zcryptor
DoppelPaymer	NetWalker	TorrentLocker
Cryptolocker	Jigsaw	Samsam
KeRanger	Bad Rabbit	Cerber
GandCrab	LeChiffre	NotPetya

Compiled from sources across the web

The WannaCry and NotPetya attacks are two ransomware attacks that together cost the world USD 14 billion dollars in losses. These two were almost catastrophic in nature, not just because of the losses caused but also because they spread like a global epidemic.

WannaCry's Worldwide Attack

WannaCry is considered to be among the first instances of a worldwide ransomware attack. It began on 12 May, 2017. In just four days, the WannaCry epidemic knocked out more than 200,000 computers (to grow later to 230,000 computers) in 150 countries. Those affected by this ransomware epidemic included critical infrastructure like factories and hospitals. No cyberattack before this had such a far-reaching effect.

Among the worst hit by WannaCry ransomware was Britain's National Health Service (NHS), where operations in 36 hospitals across the country were disrupted. Other big names of companies that were affected included FedEx, Nissan Motors, Renault SA, China National Petroleum, Deutsche Bahn, Hitachi, Sberbank of Russia, the Yancheng police department in China and the Russian Interior Ministry. Four countries that were impacted the most were Russia, Ukraine, India and Taiwan.

In India, the Gujarat Statewide Area Network reported that over 120 computers were infected by WannaCry. Hospitals in the state of Odisha, the Electricity distribution company in

West Bengal and the police departments in Andhra Pradesh and Maharashtra were also partially hit (Singhal, 2017).

Once the WannaCry ransomware infected computers over a target network by encrypting files, attackers demanded that victims pay between USD 300 and USD 600 in Bitcoin (a cryptocurrency) to decrypt their files for future use. The attackers, which included the Lazarus Group, were allegedly behind several major attacks (Orcutt, 2020). The attackers concealed their identities by converting Bitcoin into a virtual currency called Monero, which is untraceable as it does not need account details or a signup. Currencies like Monero can be used for buying goods and services on the deep web. The deep web refers to that part of the internet that is not fully accessible using standard search engines such as Google, Yahoo and Bing. According to several reports, WannaCry is still out there and may become hyperactive again.

NotPetya: The World's Biggest Ransomware Attack

Close on the heels of the WannaCry ransomware attacks came another global cyber-epidemic in the form of NotPetya. It was first identified in June 2017 and went on to cause more than two and a half times the losses that WannaCry had caused. The total estimated losses were over USD 10 billion, making this not only number one in the biggest ransomware attacks list but also among all cyberattacks in terms of damage caused.

The Petya malware was first seen in 2016. It targeted the Microsoft Windows Operating System. The Petya malware was capable of infecting the master boot record, overwriting the boot loader, and encrypting the File Allocation Table (FAT) on a target hard disk drive. The FAT is a file system which uses a table to track the clusters on a storage volume. Without using the FAT, it is not possible to access files and directories.

It is interesting to note that the name "Petya" has its origin in the 1995 James Bond film GoldenEye. In the film, Petya is one of the two Soviet weapon satellites which carry a "Goldeneye" (an atomic bomb). If the Petya malware was the equivalent of a bomb in the cyber world, the NotPetya was even more potent.

NotPetya, a variant of Petya, caused more damage than Petya by targeting business enterprises, resulting in more pain and damage even though the number of machines infected was lower than the WannaCry malware. Nevertheless, NotPetya spread to more than 65 countries, impacting top businesses.

NotPetya attacks that shook the corporate world (Kovacs, 2017)

TNT Express (Owned by FedEx)	Operations of FedEx's TNT Express unit in Europe were disrupted, with estimated losses of USD 300 million in lost earnings.
AP Moller-Maersk (Danish Shipping Giant)	Maersk was unable to process shipping orders until systems were restored, freezing revenue from several of the company's shipping container lines for weeks. Estimated losses USD 300 million.
Merck (American Pharmaceutical company)	The attack disrupted its worldwide operations, including manufacturing, research and sales. Around 40,000 computers were damaged by the ransomware. Estimated losses of USD 1 billion in damage between its equipment replacement, business outages and outside contractors brought in for remediation.
Reckitt Benckiser (Makers of Nurofen, Dettol, Durex)	The attack derailed the company's ability to manufacture and distribute products. Impact of USD 130 million on its revenue.
Nuance Communications (Conversational artificial intelligence solutions provider)	The estimated losses were over USD 15 million. The company's healthcare business was the most impacted.
Mondelez International (Owner of the UK chocolate-maker, Cadbury)	The estimated cost of the attack was over USD 150 million. Sales, distribution and financial networks were affected by the malware.

Contd.

Saint-Gobain (**French construction company**)	The attack resulted in the downtime of IT systems as well as supply chain disruptions. Total losses from the attack were estimated at around USD 387 million.
Beiersdorf (**German maker of Nivea skincare products**)	The attack affected the company's IT and telephone systems worldwide. The attack led to a shift in sales from one quarter to the next.

Next in line of major ransomware attacks are those undertaken by gangs known by the software ReEvil or Sodinokibi. The malware used by them has been described as 'highly intrusive and evasive' and is distributed through 'Ransomware-as-a-Service' (RaaS model), which means that it is available for hire.

Sodinokibi Ransomware

Sodinokibi ransomware is capable of encrypting almost any type of file, including those with the following extensions: .jpg, .jpeg, .raw, .tif, .png, .bmp, .3dm, .max, .accdb, .db, .mdb, .dwg, .dxf, .cpp, .cs, .h, .php, .asp, .rb, .java, .aaf, .aep, .aepx, .plb, .prel, .aet, .ppj, .gif and .psd (Umawing, 2019). Once the encryption is carried out, it is programmed to display a ransom demand on the screen.

First discovered in 2019, Sodinokibi ransomware caused damages that cost organisations at least USD 200 million. The targets of the malware were primarily the financial and transportation sectors. Interestingly, the malware maintained a whitelist whereby countries having friendly relations with Russia, such as Romania, Georgia, Turkmenistan, Syria, etc., could not be infected by it. It is rumoured that Sodinikibi was written by the authors who previously developed ransomware called GandCrab, which is said to be responsible for over a third of ransomware infections around the world. Ransomware attacks are often initiated through emails, spear-phishing links, attachments, remote desktop access, vulnerable websites and exploits.

One of the most high-profile cases where Sodinokibi was deployed was the 31 December 2019 attack on Travelex, the world's largest foreign exchange bureau at the time. The company's operations were disrupted because of the attack, and its offices in many countries had to conduct their business using pen and paper. The hackers made a ransom demand of USD 6 million to restore the Travelex customer data. Travelex later confirmed that no personal data of customers was compromised in the attack. Investigations revealed that Travelex had failed to patch a vulnerability in their Pulse Secure VPN servers even though warnings were issued months before (Haworth, 2020).

It was reported that Travelex had paid USD 2.3 million in Bitcoin to recover its data and restore its systems(Abbot, n.d.). A big price to pay for a small lapse.

Revil Ransomware

Over a period of three to four years, Revil became one of the most successful and dangerous cybercrime syndicates in the world. In 2020, Revil was involved in stealing a large swathe of data (one terabyte) from Grubman Shire Meiselas & Sacks (GSMS), a leading legal firm. They initially made a ransom demand of USD 21 million but doubled the demand to USD 42 million when they discovered that among the stolen data, there was information related to Donald Trump. Data stolen in the GSMS attack also included personal information related to celebrities like Madonna, Lady Gaga, Bruce Springsteen and Elton John. On the advice of the FBI, GSMS refused to pay the ransom. Some of the data was recovered through privately hired persons, but much of it is still available for sale on the deep web (Grey, 2020).

The threat actors behind the Revil ransomware strain were reported to engage in a large number of ransomware attacks that helped them generate annual revenues of over USD 100 million (Bisson, 2021). In 2021, the REvil gang pulled off a massive supply chain attack, which infected thousands of businesses with ransomware. More of this attack is covered in a later chapter on supply chain attacks.

Two notable REvil ransomware attacks were the ones which disrupted operations at Acer, one of the largest PC manufacturers in the world, and the Harris Federation, an educational academy.

The Harris Federation is a multi-academy trust based in the United Kingdom, comprising 52 primary and secondary academies in and around London. The ransomware hack of March 2021 completely disrupted the operations of the federation and forced them to temporarily disable devices given to students, suspend email services and even telephone systems.

In the same month, Acer was hit by a ransomware attack wherein threat actors claimed to be in possession of confidential documents, like financial spreadsheets, bank documents and internal communications. The ransom demanded (USD 50 million) was unprecedented and the highest ransom demand ever (Abrams, 2021).

In early 2022, the Russian Federal Security Service (FSB) announced that it had conducted raids on the infamous REvil ransomware gang and shut down its operations.

There have been several other ransomware attacks, some where large amounts of data were stolen, like Impressa (50 Terabytes) and others, like SamSam, where a ransom of USD 6 million was demanded. There is also the famous Colonial Pipeline ransomware attack that paralysed the distribution of gas on the East Coast of the US, where the loss was estimated to be USD 4.4 million (see Chapter One for more details).

There is also a ransomware called CryptoLocker. The first attacks were discovered in 2013 and reached a peak in 2017. In all, the malware is reported to have attacked over 250,000 machines by encrypting their files. CryptoLocker is estimated to have hit 5,000 organisations.

There is no argument about the fact that ransomware is among the most damaging and devastating malware in history, but surprisingly, among the list of individual malware that has caused the maximum losses in history, their rank starts at number four, as shown below:

Top 10 Malware That Caused Maximum Losses

Sl. No.	Name of Malware	Total Damage in USD
1.	Mydoom (2004)	38 billion
2.	Sobig (2003)	30 billion
3.	Klez (2001)	19.8 billion
4.	NotPetya (2017)	10 billion
5.	WannCry (2016)	4 billion
6.	ILOVEYOU (2000s)	4 billion
7.	Zeus (2007)	3 billion
8.	CodeRed (2001)	2.4 billion
9.	Slammer (2003)	1.2 billion
10.	CryptoLocker (2013)	665 million

Source: https://www.hp.com/us-en/shop/tech-takes/top-ten-worst-computer-viruses-in-history

A closer analysis of the above data shows that if we consider only the past decade, ransomware emerges at the top of the list of malware causing the greatest losses. Ransomware is the biggest cyber threat to businesses, and it is not easing up anytime soon.

7

Sneaking Through: Prominent Supply Chain Attacks

The threat of a supply chain cyberattack significantly enhances the cyber risk faced by organisations today. In an increasingly connected world, cyber threats and attacks can emanate from the weakest partner systems in a supply chain and can lead to major attacks across sectors, like the information technology sector, manufacturing companies, large retailers, the financial sector and practically any industry that depends on a chain of suppliers or third parties to accomplish their goals and objectives.

There is an age-old adage saying that the strength of a chain is limited to its weakest link. This is true even in the cyber world. When cybercriminals find it hard to penetrate strong and well-protected organisations, they look at the organisations' suppliers, vendors, contractors, service providers and other third parties that may have access to the organisation's systems and do not have the same level of security in place.

The Target attack (covered in chapter 4) showed us how hackers used the credentials given to an HVAC contractor to get into Target's IT network to pull off one of the most shocking cyberattacks in history. The supplier or vendor base of an organisation is built up of firms that are usually smaller than the organisation. Hiring their services organizations can provide specialised services at lower costs, thereby making them more competitive. However, their costs are lower also on account of the smaller operations that they run. This means that their investments in areas like cybersecurity are lower, keeping them more vulnerable. To derive operational efficiencies of organisations, offer connectivity and access to their systems to their supply chain partners. Cybercriminals are well aware of this and know that it is easier to target large organisations via their supply chain partners.

It is one thing for large organisations to monitor their own cybersecurity, but to do the same across the supply chain is quite a daunting task. Hence, cybercriminals are increasingly choosing to launch attacks through the supply chain, where they encounter fewer security mechanisms, can remain inconspicuous and use sly, subtle, or surreptitious means to break in.

A supply chain can also be considered a system of activities engaged in handling, distributing, manufacturing and processing goods or providing the required services to move resources from a vendor into the hands of the ultimate consumer.

Organisations have actively digitised their processes in the past decade to enhance efficiencies and improve productivity. IT plays a key role in managing supply chain operations by integrating functions and business processes across entities and geographies.

A supply chain cyberattack aims to cause harm to an organisation by targeting weaker and more vulnerable elements in the supply chain.

Log4j Attack

Hackers can launch supply chain attacks in multiple ways, all of which are based upon exploiting security weaknesses across the supply chain. Common methods include hardware and software having malicious code, exploiting weak endpoint security, Application Programming Interfaces (APIs), stolen certificates, eavesdropping, malware preinstalled on devices, password-breaking techniques and more. In recent times, one of the methods used by hackers for maximum impact is inserting malicious code in software updates. Prominent attacks using this technique were the SolarWinds attack (detailed in Chapter One and Chapter Three), Log4j and Kaseya. Updates are an important part of the software life cycle.

The Apache Log4j Project is among the most popular pieces of open-source software. It provides logging capabilities for Java applications. Java is a widely used platform and network-centric language that is employed across a range of products, such as cloud solutions and web servers. A critical vulnerability in the Log4j shell was discovered and began to be actively exploited in December 2021, making applications in each of these products vulnerable to exploitation through the Log4Shell vulnerability. What it needed was just a simple malicious code injection.

News about this vulnerability spread fast and soon had the hacker community in a frenzy to exploit the vulnerability. The impact was widespread, and security researchers estimated around ten million Log4Shell exploitation attempts every hour (Kost, 2023). Industries that were impacted were retail, financial services and manufacturing, but given the usage across industries, it was only a matter of time before other sectors, like healthcare, government, etc., were affected. In a regional context, the most impacted regions were the United States, the United Kingdom, Germany, Turkey and the Netherlands.

Apache Log4j is the most popular logging framework used on the internet. It is used by millions of applications and even by cloud services like Apple, Google, Microsoft and Cloudflare, as well as platforms like Twitter, VMware and Stream. Hence, potentially, it can cause damage to millions of organisations around the world. Many organisations may not even know how many applications they are using that rely on Log4j.

The matter was taken very seriously by the Cybersecurity and Infrastructure Security Agency (CISA), USA, which issued an Emergency Directive on December 17 that directed US federal government agencies to mitigate, patch or remove all applications and services affected by the Log4j exploits (Kerner, 2022).

Kaseya VSA Attack

Another supply chain attack that shocked and baffled businesses and governments around the globe is commonly called the Kaseya VSA attack. Kaseya VSA is a Remote Monitoring and

Management software that helps monitor, manage and secure any endpoint from anywhere. Kaseya is an American software company that develops software for managing networks, systems and information technology infrastructure. The reason this cyberattack is unique is because the threat actors (REvil) exploited a zero-day vulnerability to launch a ransomware attack. The modus operandi was to use a Kaseya update to deploy ransomware.

Kaseya provides its software to several third-party service providers that manage IT for other companies, often small and medium-sized businesses. Therefore, by using Kaseya's software as a vehicle, the attackers gained access to over a thousand companies and government organisations. One of the victims was a Swedish grocery chain that had to close hundreds of stores. Kaseya is also among the biggest ransomware supply chain attacks, considering the aggregate ransom demand of USD 70 million made by the hackers.

The use of third-party and open-source software is today a part of every software project. Even software vendors use open-source code as it speeds up the development process. Studies suggest that 80 per cent of all code in modern applications comes from open sources. Another astounding fact is that, on average, there are 203 open-source dependencies, which could translate into countless vulnerabilities (Beg, 2023). This is among the key reasons for the growth of supply chain attacks in recent times.

Technology platforms and even supply chain architecture have moved to greater dependence on third parties for running their operations. These third parties may further be dependent on fourth and nth parties to provide their products and services. Hence, organisations are ever more dependent on third-party software, which makes supply chain attacks an attractive attack vector for hackers.

JP Morgan Chase, an American multinational financial services company, was delivered a shock by hackers who stole usernames and passwords for 76 million households and 7 billion business accounts through an unmonitored website developed by a third party for them in support of charity. Hackers broke through this to get inside core systems (Beg, 2023).

A supply chain cyberattack on the diamond industry sounds farfetched. In February 2022, a hacker group allegedly from Iran conducted a supply chain attack via Israeli software used in the diamond industry. They deployed a wiper software called Fantasy. This deadly wiper either wipes all files on disk or wipes all files with extensions on a list of as many as 682 extensions. Though this malware is potent, recovery is possible.

Applied Materials Attack

Applied Material is a semiconductor company that grew from a small start-up into one of the most admired companies in the world. They have contributed to the growth and evolution of the electronics industry, and it is said that they put the "silicon" in Silicon Valley (Applied Materials, n.d.).

A business partner of Applied Materials suffered a supply chain attack in February 2023. The attack disrupted production schedules at Applied Materials, leading to delays in supplies. While Applied Materials did not name the business partner, it admitted that the disruption would cost the company USD 250 million in the forthcoming quarter.

It was around this time that MKS Instruments, an industrial equipment supplier, suffered a ransomware attack and could have been the business partner that Applied Materials refused to confirm.

If MKS Instrument was actually the source of the supply chain attack, then security experts opined that it could be due to a worldwide campaign against VMware ESXi servers, which was targeting established but unpatched vulnerabilities. It is reported that as part of this hackers' campaign, at least 3,200 servers around the world were affected. The hackers have been actively demanding ransom and threatening the exposure of data (Ikeda, 2023).

Who would have expected the semiconductor industry to be the target of a ransomware attack? While there were attempts in the past to target the semiconductor industry in 2022 as well, mainly through supply chain attacks, none caused as much damage as the MKS Instruments attack.

Airbus Cyberattack

Airbus Industrie is Europe's premier aircraft-manufacturing consortium, formed in 1970 to make short to medium-range and high-capacity jetliners. The company is an attractive target to cybercriminals who work on behalf of adversaries to steal details of design and technology, which is of great strategic value.

Airbus has a complex network of suppliers, which includes large companies to smaller suppliers. In 2017 and 2018, hackers successfully breached Airbus through a series of supply chain attacks via suppliers like Rolls-Royce and French technology company Expleo. In all, the hackers (allegedly Chinese) targeted at least four Airbus vendors and partners in their effort to reach their target. Their objective was to steal technical documents and confidential information related to the engines of the Airbus military transport plane A400M. The hackers' actions showed that they further evinced interest in specific technical documents linked to the certification process for different parts of the Airbus aircraft, as well as in the propulsion systems for the Airbus A350 passenger jet and its avionics systems that control the plane (NDTV, 2019).

The attacks were carried out with a great degree of expertise and sophistication by breaking into the Virtual Private Network (VPN) links that supplier companies use to establish secure links to connect to Airbus's systems.

These attacks show that it is not only smaller suppliers with weaker security that are targeted but also those larger and more strategic ones that have access to privileged and confidential information. It is therefore important that security standards must be applied across a supply chain network and that intrusions are detected early through continuous monitoring.

Cyber supply chain risk can arise from several sources. National Institute of Standards and Technology (NIST), USA provides a list of examples of best practices related to managing the Cyber Supply Chain (NIST, n.d.).

- Every Request for Proposal (RFP) and contract with supply chain partners must detail security requirements
- Onboarding a supplier should include a security team working with the supplier to ensure that any vulnerabilities and security gaps are addressed
- Strong action to be taken in the event of the use of counterfeit products by vendors
- All parts and components should be purchased from approved vendors
- Secure Software Lifecycle Development Programs and training for all engineers in the life cycle must be implemented
- Source code must be available for all purchased software
- Software and hardware have a security handshake and authentication processes
- Establish automated manufacturing and testing regimes
- Track and trace programs which establish provenance of all parts, components and systems.
- Every component must have identity data for each assembly and automatically links the component identity data to sourcing information. Maintenance of Software Bill of Materials (SBOMs)
- Cybersecurity practices should be a part of every supply chain partner's operating procedure
- Legacy support for end-of-life products and platforms supplied
- Security controls to be implemented on access by service vendors are enforced. Access to hardware/software is limited to selected vendors. Hardware vendors must be limited to mechanical systems with no access to control systems. All vendors should be authorised and escorted at all times.

Source: NIST

The JBS Foods Attack

One of the most disruptive and disturbing supply chain cyberattacks ever was targeted at JBS Foods, the world's largest meat processing company. JBS has over 150 plants in

15 countries and employs over 150,000 people worldwide. Among its customers are major supermarkets and the fast-food outlet McDonald's. The ransomware attack forced JBS to shut down beef and poultry processing plants on four continents. The attack led to shortages of meat supplies for consumers, especially in the USA and Australia. A ransom demand of USD 11 million was made by the hackers and paid by JBS. The company suspended all affected IT systems as soon as the attack was detected. Fortunately, their backup servers were not hacked (BBC, 2022).

Supply chain cyberattacks can be considered the Achilles heel of cybersecurity and must be dealt with great seriousness to avoid any untoward cyber incidents. The recent increase in cyberattacks and ransomware incidents underlines the need for a new approach to the security of the supply chain network.

8
The World's Biggest Cyberheists

A heist in the physical world involves burglary or robbery, an event in which money, jewellery, or art is stolen. A cyberheist refers to a theft or robbery, often of money, that takes place in cyberspace or on the internet.

Cyberheists are not the handiwork of 'lone wolf' operators. More often, they are planned and executed by specially assembled teams comprising members who are specialists in their field of operation. At a minimum, at least five roles (listed below) need to be played during a cyberheist, and the team members must be equipped with knowledge and skills to carry out their part of an operation. Depending on the scale and complexity of a particular heist, more members may be inducted.

Cyberheist Team

Entry strategy specialist	Responsible for determining and executing an entry strategy using social engineering, phishing and/or other techniques
Domain Specialist	Responsible for identifying and using domain knowledge to conduct the operation
Technology Specialist	Responsible for the technical execution of the heist
Money Manager	Responsible for moving the money quickly through several accounts and currencies across countries right up to the ultimate beneficiary
Team Leader	Responsible for planning and execution of the entire operation

The Bank of Bangladesh Cyberheist

Cyberheists are often about stealing money. It is not surprising that the hackers' primary targets should be banks. The Bangladesh Bank cyberheist is one such case, where hackers in February 2016 attempted to transfer as much as USD one billion from the Federal Reserve Bank of New York, where the Bank of Bangladesh has an account. The Bank of Bangladesh is the central bank of Bangladesh and maintains an account with the Federal Reserve Bank of New York to deposit, maintain and transfer foreign currency reserve of Bangladesh.

A total of 35 fraudulent instructions for transferring money via the SWIFT network were issued by the hackers. This set in motion the transfer of money to accounts in various countries such as the Philippines (USD 101 million) and Sri Lanka (USD 20 million).

A spelling mistake in some of the instructions by the hackers aroused suspicions at The Federal Reserve Bank of New York, which blocked the transfer of USD 850 million (Schram, 2016).

A portion of the money (around USD 18 million) was recovered out of the USD 101 million that was transferred into accounts with the Rizal Commercial Banking Corporation (RCBC) from what were found to belong to fictitious identities. These funds were converted to Philippine pesos through a foreign exchange broker, returned to the RCBC and consolidated in a single account belonging to a Chinese-Filipino businessman.

Funds that were moved to Sri Lanka (USD 20 million) were credited to the account of Shalika Foundation, a Sri Lanka-based private limited company. In the transfer request, the hackers yet again made the mistake of spelling the word 'Foundation' as 'Fundation'. This aroused suspicion at Deutsche Bank, a routing bank, which stopped the transaction and sought clarifications from the Bank of Bangladesh. Eventually, the Bank of Bangladesh recovered the full amount of USD 20 million from Sri Lanka.

The perpetrators of this cyberheist (suspected to be from North Korea) could have been aided by insiders who were aware of some security loopholes in the SWIFT system. Earlier, in 2013, there was a similar cyberheist at the Sonali Bank of Bangladesh, where an amount of USD 250,000 was stolen.

Investigations into the cyberheist revealed that some malware was installed in the bank's systems sometime in January 2016. The heist involved social engineering, insider help and deep knowledge of banking systems and procedures related to money transfers. The cyberheist resulted in the loss of $81 million to the Bank of Bangladesh.

Other Bank Cyberheists

Another state-owned Indian bank, the Union Bank of India, was allegedly targeted by North Korean-linked hackers who stole an amount of USD 170 million in July 2016. Fortunately, the money was recovered after investigators were able to reverse the charges, which were made through another attempt on the SWIFT system.

In August 2018, Cosmas Bank, one of India's oldest banks, was the victim of a cyberheist. The attack happened in two stages, from August 10–13. The hackers used malware on the bank's ATM server to steal the credit card information of customers, along with SWIFT codes required for transactions. In the first attempt, they transferred nearly USD 11.5 million, followed by USD 2 million in the second attempt.

The money was transmitted to New York banks, Australian and Taiwanese financial institutions and two Cambodian banks. Funds were subsequently transferred to Hong Kong through fraudulent SWIFT transactions.

In all, USD 12.5 million was stolen in seven hours through thousands of ATM transactions (withdrawn through cloned debit cards) in India and 28 other countries.

A year later, an Indian magistrate court convicted eleven accused, and sentenced them to different periods of imprisonment and imposed fines of varying amounts.

The Malaysian Central Bank was the target of a USD 390 million cyberheist in March 2018. Again, the modalities were the use of fraudulent wire transfers initiated using the SWIFT system.

The repeated heists using the SWIFT (the Society for Worldwide Interbank Financial Telecommunication) network raised the shackles among international financial institutions regarding the security of money transfers. While security updates were released by the SWIFT cooperative and participating banks at their end, a long-term solution in the form of using Blockchain technology has been under consideration. Blockchains maintain immutable distributed ledgers to record transactions and operate via consensus mechanisms that require agreement between participants. This means that data is validated before registering a transaction. SWIFT has yet to implement the use of blockchain technology but is likely to do so in the near future, subject to successful trials.

Mt. Gox Cyberheist

Cryptocurrencies are digital or virtual currencies that are secured by cryptography. They use blockchain technologies, which should make it impossible to steal or counterfeit. However, hackers have still found ways to conduct cyberheists.

Mt. Gox was a Bitcoin exchange based in Tokyo, Japan. The Mt. Gox cyberheist is considered the greatest cyberheist in history, where over 850k Bitcoin was stolen between 2011 and 2014. The impact caused was massive: USD 460 million stolen by hackers, and another USD 27.4 million missing from its bank accounts. Inevitably, Mt. Gox had to file for bankruptcy soon after (McMillan, 2014).

Mt. Gox survived an attack in June 2011 and recovered to win back the confidence of customers and went on to become the world's most popular Bitcoin exchange. Mark Karpeles, the 28-year-old majority owner and CEO of Mt. Gox, soon began to be known as the King of Bitcoin, with over 70 per cent of all Bitcoin (BTC) transactions worldwide being conducted on his exchange by early 2014.

Soon after, on 7 February 2014, Mt. Gox halted all Bitcoin withdrawals, and from thereon, it was downhill. It was reported that 200,000 Bitcoins were found, but it was a case of 'too-little-too-late'. The fall of Mt. Gox was attributed to the heist but also to fraud and mismanagement.

Alexey Bilyuchenko, 43, and Aleksandr Verner, 29, both Russian nationals, were charged with conspiring to launder approximately 647,000 Bitcoins from their hack of Mt. Gox(DOJ, 2023). Despite the convictions, Mt. Gox remains the most inconclusive cryptoheist in history. Mark Karpeles was arrested following the investigation. USD 500,000 was seized from the company's bank accounts, and a Trustee was appointed to oversee giving money back to victims after the sale of Mt. Gox BTC.

Bitcoin companies today use a combination of hot and cold wallets to secure Bitcoin and minimise losses in the event of a cyberheist. All Bitcoin is stored in an exchange's cold wallet and is manually transferred to a hot wallet as and when required. If an exchange's server is hacked, the attacker can only steal money from the hot wallet.

A Curious Cyberheist

Hackers are known to be innovative, but they are also capable of getting through and conducting their cyber raids when faced with formidable and sophisticated technology platforms. A web hosting company, Linode, was sued by Bitcoin companies for storing and managing their hot wallets. Hackers carried out a cyberheist and stole 46,000 Bitcoins. The two losers were Bitcoinia (43,000 stolen) and Bitcoin.cx (3,000 stolen).

In August 2021, a major cyberheist was reported related to the theft of nearly USD 600 million worth of digital tokens. This is regarded as one of the greatest cryptocurrency thefts ever. The hacker exploited a security loophole in the network of Poly Network, a Decentralised Finance (DeFi) platform.

From here, the story becomes more curious, as the hacker not only kept a public communication channel open with the victim but also went ahead and returned everything that he had stolen except for USD 33 million in Tether (USDT) that had been frozen by the issuers. Tether (USDT) is a cryptocurrency stablecoin pegged to the US dollar and backed one hundred per cent by Tether's reserves. His actions earned the hacker the sobriquet 'Mr. White Hat". He was also offered a USD 500,000 prize for returning all stolen cash, as well as a job offer to become Poly Network's senior security officer (CoinTelegraph, 2023).

KuCoin Cyberheist

KuCoin is a cryptocurrency exchange located in Singapore. One night in September 2020, security personnel observed unusual activity in several hot wallets. To secure themselves from any criminal act, they moved all the assets from compromised hot wallets to cold wallets. This activity took about two hours, but they could not prevent the hackers from withdrawing about USD 285 million in multiple cryptocurrencies.

Among the suspects was the Lazarus group (a North Korean syndicate), who could have gotten a hold of the private keys of hot wallets. While this remained in the realm of speculation, the KuCoin CEO Johny Lyu promised publicly to reimburse the money stolen in this heist. It is interesting to note that Lyu lived up to his promise and made good on the money to their owners. No wonder KuCoin says that they are the most trusted and secure trading platform for Bitcoin and other cryptocurrencies in the world (KuCoin, n.d.).

Wormhole is an open-source software tool that mediates cryptocurrency transactions. Its function is to enable users to move tokens between the Ethereum and Solana networks. Wormhole has a repository on GitHub (a platform that acts as a cloud-based service for software development and version control). Just prior to the heist, the development team placed new code fixing a vulnerability, but the hackers were one step ahead and exploited the vulnerability before the changes were affected. The hackers were successful in bypassing transaction verification on the Solana network side and managed to steal the equivalent of USD 334 million. Wormhole publicly offered USD 10 million to the hackers to return the money and provide them with the details of how they managed the heist. The hackers, who remain unknown, however, did not oblige (Starikova, n.d.).

Coincheck Heist

Over time, Japan has emerged as a cryptocurrency hub. Coincheck is one of Japan's largest cryptocurrency exchanges. In a major cyberheist in 2018, hackers managed to steal nearly half a billion US dollars. More precisely, the loss was USD 496 million, which the hackers stole using tactics similar to the KuCoin cyber heist by gaining access to private keys of Coincheck hot wallets along with the use of other malware. The exchange had to shut down for a brief period and promised to reimburse clients whose funds were stolen. The hackers remained undetected(Tsuchiya & Hiramoto, 2021).

Sky Mavis Cyberheist

Blockchain technology is considered robust and secure among different choices of platforms. However, even blockchain is not immune to social engineering attacks. Using social engineering methods, hackers target and manipulate human beings to gain private information, access or other valuable assets, including cryptocurrency.

Sky Mavis is a Vietnamese studio founded in 2017 that went on to make Axie Infinity, a game that uses Non-Fungible Tokens (NFTs) to reward players financially as an incentive to play more. This encouraged players to act more like owners and employees rather than users. The Ronin Blockchain Network was an offshoot of this venture, which was a play-to-earn game that allowed players to buy the in-game currency, which was called Smooth Love Potion (SLP). In March 2022, hackers, using a combination of spyware and social engineering, stole a record USD 540 million.

First, for the social engineering, Sky Mavis employees were targeted probably via LinkedIn with a 'job offer' in the form of a PDF file which was preloaded with spyware. Through this technique, the hackers managed to get four out of five network private validator keys. In all, five keys were required to get access to the company's assets. They got the crucial fifth key through a mistake of the company, which had given authorisation permissions to sign off on transactions and forgot to revoke them. It took Sky Mavis three months to recover and relaunch its blockchain platform and begin the process of reimbursing its impacted players(Starikova, n.d.).

An 'Unlimited Operation' Cyberheist

If there was a cyber shocker that takes the cake, here is one that sent shock waves around the world. The fact that cybercriminals strike across the world is not new, but when they conduct a part cyber, part physical operation across 26 countries, we are talking about a level of collaboration among cyber thieves that's never been seen before.

In a major cyberheist in 2013, cybercriminals stole USD 45 million through 40,500 transactions in 10 hours in 27 countries. An operation like this is known as an 'unlimited operation' in cybercrime circles, and it made headlines around the world.

Eight people who were a part of the New York cell of the cybercrime were charged for their role in the crime for allegedly lifting USD 2.8 million in cash from ATMs.

The cybercrime syndicate infiltrated credit card processors' computer networks, specifically seeking information related to prepaid debit cards, a tool used often by employers and aid organisations. Once inside the system, they removed the card limits as fixed by the banks. (BBC, 2013a, 2013b)

The cyber thieves then distributed the debit card numbers to its feet-on-the-street associates called 'cashers', who loaded other magnetic stripe cards, like gift cards, with the stolen information. The cashers were then given the required PIN numbers so that they could go to ATMs and withdraw as much cash as possible.

The Citibank Heist of 1994

The first major cyberheist goes back all the way to 1994 when Vladimir Levin and his team of hackers operating out of St. Petersburg hacked into Citibank's telephone and computer systems and stole USD 10 million. At this time, Citibank was embracing digital systems, limiting the growth of its physical branches and adding more electronic systems to lower costs. They were also implementing a new international electronic money transfer system. Levin's team stole account credentials, such as account numbers and passwords, by intercepting them when they were being communicated to Citibank customer service personnel on the phone. Using the stolen credentials, the hackers initiated an electronic money transfer to a number of accounts around the world. Levin was eventually caught and sentenced to three years in prison. Out of the USD 10 million he stole, all the money except USD 400,000 was recovered. This first cyberheist left the financial world shocked and was a forerunner to more cyberheists that were to take place in future.

9

Outsmarted: Top IoT Attacks

Smart devices, also referred to as the Internet of Things (IoT), have transformed our lives, whether at home, at work or even when we are travelling. While IoT devices have given us numerous benefits in terms of efficiency, time savings, productivity and convenience, they have also increased our security risks. The smarter the device, the higher the level of vulnerability to cyberattacks.

Smart devices today are everywhere. From the ubiquitous smartphone that can perform multiple functions, and wearables like smartwatches, to specific life-sustaining devices such as pacemakers and implantable defibrillators, smart devices are invading our homes and workplaces. The adoption of smart devices has been unbelievably rapid, and the IoT landscape is exploding with various devices.

A smart device is an electronic gadget or machine that can interact, connect and share information with other smart devices. Through the use of advanced technologies like artificial intelligence and machine learning, these smart devices can perform simple to highly sophisticated functions.

IoT device designers have focused their efforts on providing users with the functionality that they need, with security taking a backseat. To get to the market quickly, device-makers have often not given security the importance that it deserves. Thus, today, there are billions of IoT devices being used across sectors that lack built-in safeguards. To add to the problem, these devices are often unmanaged, making them an ideal entry point for a hacker to launch a cyberattack.

When it comes to risks from cyberattacks, connected medical devices top the list. Many devices still operate on old and unsupported operating systems, which remain unpatched, even as cyberattacks continue to grow in the healthcare sector.

A warning issued by Singapore's Cyber Security Agency (CSA) suggests that critical IoT devices are potential targets in ransomware attacks, with hackers recognising that they could cause harm by infecting these devices, which could lead to significant harm with life-threatening consequences. The CSA has launched a program where it is working with the Ministry of Health, the Health Sciences Authority and Integrated Health Information Systems on implementing a Cybersecurity Labelling Scheme for Medical Devices. These devices are often connected to the hospital and home networks in the intranet and internet. While there are benefits of connectivity, like real-time patient monitoring, they also increase cybersecurity risks and could compromise patients' personal information, clinical data or treatment protocols, which may affect the patient's health outcomes(CSA, 2022). While there have been several hospitals that have been targeted with ransomware attacks, there have been no reports of direct attacks on medical devices so far. However, it must be noted that according to Check Point Research, cyberattacks against healthcare organisations across the world increased by 74 per cent in 2022(IEC, 2023).

The Mirai Botnet, which was used to launch among the biggest DDoS attacks of all time (see Chapter 3), resulted in a host of major organisations that included the likes of Twitter, Netflix, CNN and the Guardian, among several others, becoming inaccessible for several hours. Using a botnet of Internet of Things devices, hackers attacked the Domain Services Provider Dyn's servers. The Mirai malware infects smart devices that run on Argonaut RISC Core (ARC) embedded system processors and converts them into a network of remotely controlled bots. The Mirai malware was used by its creators, Josiah White, Paras Jha and Dalton Norman, to create a botnet. It grew to an estimated 145,000 IoT devices and evolved to perform large-scale attacks. Mirai works like a self-propagating worm that replicates itself, and after infecting one device it locates another vulnerable IoT

chaining three vulnerabilities, they could remotely hack into a Tesla car, turn off the lights, blow the horn, open the boot, activate the wipers and tamper with the infotainment system. Tesla cars are among the most coveted acquisitions for car enthusiasts. Tesla representatives maintained that the hackers cannot start or shut down the car, control the steering wheel or accelerate and brake. Tesla is reportedly working on making patches available to fix vulnerabilities, and the updates should be pushed to cars soon(Franceschi-Biccheirai. Lorenzo, 2023).

In Milwaukee, USA, Samantha and Lamont Westmoreland were shocked and terrified to know that their smart home had been hacked. The hackers had taken control of the connected devices and demonstrated it to the couple by playing disturbing music from the video system at a high volume even as they talked to them via a camera in the kitchen. To further demonstrate their control, they increased the room temperature to 90 degrees Fahrenheit by exploiting the thermostat. Initially, the couple tried to change their passwords to regain control, but when that did not work, they changed their network ID after finding that their Wi-Fi system had been hacked.

In another cyberattack in November 2016—when it is freezing cold in Finland—hackers launched a DDoS attack and successfully managed to turn off the heating of two buildings in the city of Lappeenranta. By flooding the heating controllers with unmanageable traffic, the hackers caused them to continually reboot the system so that the heating never actually kicked in. The discomfort caused to the occupants of the two buildings was immense, as temperatures in Finland dip well below freezing at that time of year.

Can your car spy on you? Cars are getting smarter by the day. Present-day cars come equipped with cameras and all sorts of other advanced software. They can collect personal information from how you interact with your car, the internet services you use in your car, such as Google Maps, as well as other information captured by the car's voice-activated applications. Experts believe that smart automobiles could be a major threat to privacy.

When you set up a coffee machine, you seldom imagine that details of your identity and bank account can be stolen. Smart coffee machines that are connected to the internet can be controlled via apps that are installed on your mobile phone. Users can also give voice commands to the coffee machines through virtual assistant software such as Amazon's Alexa.

Beware when you buy a smart car or install a smart coffee machine or anything smart for that matter, as it may also be a security threat.

10

Swindlers Inc.: Top Scams, Cons and Dirty Tricks

The digital world has become a playground for scammers and swindlers. They weaponise deception using a combination of technology and psychologically manipulating millions of trusting people. The best defence against cyber scams is not from law enforcement agencies but from knowledge and awareness of scams and scamming methods.

Swindlers or scammers have only one objective: stealing your money. Every year, millions of people worldwide lose billions of dollars to cyber fraud and scams. In 2021 alone, the Internet Crime Complaint Centre (IC3) of the FBI received 847, 376 reports, with a reported loss of USD 6.9 billion in the US alone. At a global level, The Global Anti Scam Alliance, in its annual Global State of Scam Report (2020), stated that USD 47.8 billion was lost, and the number of reported scams increased from 139 million in 2019 to 266 million in 2020 (GlobeNewsWire, 2021).

A scam is a fraudulent or deceptive act, scheme, or operation. Cyber scams are those scams that are carried out online. Internet scamming is among the fastest growing in the genre of cybercrimes on a worldwide basis. Swindlers and scammers are everywhere on the internet, and statistics suggest that one in ten people in the US fall victim to a scam. This goes to show that scamming has become a big-time business now, with cyber-scamming being the fastest-growing among various types of scams. In this chapter, we will examine how cyber scams, cons and swindles are planned and executed.

How do scammers trick millions into losing billions? To understand a successful scam from beginning to end, we need to examine the steps and stages involved. Scams do not happen by accident; they are carefully planned operations. The first step is a devious plan, which involves the selection of potential victims, understanding ways to win their trust and then pulling off the trick. The next step is to lay the bait (or hook), which typically preys on peoples' weaknesses such as greed, fear and lust. The scammers often contact people through phone calls, emails and text messages to 'dangle the bait'. The scammer can also post ads on websites or on social media to bring their proposition to the attention of the victims. A scammer's bait or trap is a falsehood that sounds a lot like the truth. At this stage, the scammer is clear in terms of what they want the victim to do in response to the trap or bait they havelaid for them. The professional scammer rolls out his plan. A scammer executes their plan hundreds of times a day and knows that their 'hit' percentage will be less than 10 to 15 per cent, or maybe even less than that. Once they have the victim hooked, the scammer engages in establishing trust with the victim. Scammers may, at times, go further by offering a small payout as a demonstration of the scheme's purported effectiveness. Once the confidence of the victims is obtained, the final act, in the form of a manufactured crisis, is brought into play, thus forcing the victims to make an immediate decision, which usually involves paying an amount of money or parting with personal information that the scammer then uses to steal the victim's money.

A scam can take the form of a short con or a quick swindle, where it is all over in a matter of seconds or minutes. There is also the long con, which unfolds over weeks and months, often involving a team of scammers and a sophisticated scheme that allows scammers to remain undetected during the period of the scam.

Business Email Compromise Scam

The Business Email Compromise (BEC) scam is an example of a short con. FACC AG is an Austrian company in the aerospace and defence industry. In January 2016, an employee of the company received what he thought was an instruction from his CEO, Walter Stephan, to transfer an amount of 42 million euros to another account as part of an 'acquisition project'. The employee followed the instructions, not knowing that it was a scam. When the fraud was discovered, FACC fired the employee as well as the Chief Financial Officer.

Following the FACC incident, a month later, a Belgian bank became a victim of a similar scam. A Crelan Bank employee received a spoofed email, which appeared as though it came from the CEO of the bank, asking to transfer a large amount to an account that was controlled by the scamster. The employee did what was asked of him, and all hell broke loose. While the amount and reason for the transfer were not revealed by the bank, the incident resulted in an overall loss of 75.6 million euros.

The FTX Scam

The long con is an elaborately laid out scam, which is planned in a way that allows scamsters to remain undetected, and their fraudulent activity continues over a long period of time. FTX Exchange was a leading centralised cryptocurrency exchange, specialising in derivates and other leveraged products. In July 2021, it was the world's third-largest cryptocurrency exchange. Sam Bankman-Fried, a young American entrepreneur, was the founder and CEO of the exchange, which reached great heights and then plunged when news of the scam broke.

Founded in 2018, FTX became the largest digital currency exchange platform for buying and selling cryptocurrencies. The exchange also allowed clients to create their own wallets and store cryptocurrencies on their own using either software or hardware, which was not part of the platform.

FTX used aggressive marketing campaigns, promising higher yields to its customers than normal bank rates. They also grew their business through the acquisition of competing platforms like Liquid Global, LedgerX and Blockfolio. Enthused by their success, venture capital companies invested close to two billion dollars in the exchange. By January 2022, FTX was valued at USD 32 billion.

Everything came crashing down in November 2022 when a gigantic fraud involving the loss of billions of dollars for customers and investors was discovered.

Sam Bankman-Fried started a trading firm, Alameda Research, in 2017, which became central to the massive fraud. It was discovered that customer funds deposited with FTX went to accounts controlled by Alameda Research instead of FTX. Alameda's need for money to run its trading business was a big reason for this.

Just before the collapse of FTX, Binance, a cryptocurrency exchange platform, agreed to buy out FTX. However, the deal fell through when the news of the problem of mishandling customer funds became public.

Binance and other customers started to sell their FTT tokens, and as the value of the FTTs dropped, customers started to withdraw their funds. This mass withdrawal led to FTX losing billions of dollars. Even after disposing of Almeida's assets, there was a gap of USD 8 billion in terms of funds required and funds available.

What was shocking was that FTX and its related entities did not produce annual balance sheets as required by financial regulations. FTX's own balance sheets were never audited. There was total opaqueness all around—for customers, other stakeholders and regulatory authorities.

Investigations also revealed that Bankman-Fried diverted FTX funds to buy personal luxury items, run big advertising campaigns and make political donations. He was tried and indicted on several criminal charges, including wire fraud, money laundering and securities fraud.

Bankman-Fried was arrested and released on a bond of USD 250 million, the biggest in history. By January 2023, USD five billion out of the missing USD 8 billion was recovered in cash and liquid assets (Reiff, 2023). Sam Bankman-Fried has since been convicted and faces more than 100 years in prison on seven charges related to the fall of his crypto empire (Sigalos, 2023).

Scams are all about confidence tricks. Confidence tricks exploit victims by playing with a combination of the victim's trust, innocence, compassion, vanity, confidence, irresponsibility and greed. Scamsters are ready to go to any extent to gain people's trust and then defraud them. They leave their victims in a state of shock and loss, with no one to blame except themselves. There are hundreds of ways in which scamsters ply their trade and even conjure up thousands of ploys to con their victims. The strongest defences against scams are awareness, alertness and good sense so that when confronted with schemes that sound attractive, demand urgent action on your behalf or lure you into sharing personal information, you do not get carried away.

Fifty Different Types of Scams

Here is a primer on fifty different types of scams. The knowledge of these can help save you from difficult and unwanted situations.

1. The Nigerian Prince Scam

This is one of the oldest scams, which plays on the greed of an individual. Typically, an email is received by the victim that says that a wealthy Nigerian prince would like to share his wealth in return for some assistance to access the inheritance. Victims are asked to make an advance payment (a small fee) or share their personal information to get their reward. After receiving the advance payment or personal details, the scamsters simply disappear. Nigerian Prince email scams still rake in over $700,000 a year (Leonhaordt, 2019).

Example of Nigerian Price scam email: (Grigutyte, 2023)

> Dear Sir,
> I am prince from Nigeria. Your help would be very appreciated.
> I want to transfer all of my fortune outside if Nigeria due to a frozen account,
> If you could be so kind and transfer small sum of 3 500 USD to my account,
> I would be able to unfreeze my account and transfer my money outside of
> Nigeria. To repay your kindness, I will send 1 000 000 USD to your account.
>
> Please contact me to proceed
>
> Prince

Source: https://nordvpn.com/blog/nigerian-prince-scam/

2. The '419' Fraud

Section 419 of the Nigerian Criminal Code deals with scams and frauds carried out by offenders. In this type of scam, the scamster contacts the potential victim and asks them to help with some administration fees required to move large sums of money between countries. In return for the advance fee, the victim is promised a large sum of money. Victims are also asked to provide details of their bank accounts to facilitate payments of the promised funds, which the fraudsters could also use for withdrawing money.

Example of a 419 Advance Fee email:

> We are the Pay Settlement Commison (PSC) been authorized by the FTC and DOJ to pay out scammed Victims. We are incharge of the New settlement paid by MoneyGram for $125 million announced by the FTC and the Department of Justice (DOJ). The settlement payout has been authorized to be compensated to does scammed Victims who wired – and lost – money to a scammer through MoneyGram starting from 2009.
>
> You have been selected has part of the scammed Victims to be compensated for a payout of $4.1million.
>
> Get back to us for further instructions.
>
> We will wait for your response.

Source: https://nordvpn.com/blog/nigerian-prince-scam/

3. The Lottery, Fake Prize and Sweepstakes Scam

Among the most common types of cyber scams is the lottery scam. The victims typically get a call or email saying the magical words "you have won". The winnings could be money, a car, or anything that holds great value.

A study revealed that nearly 60 per cent of the respondents even identified the solicitations as likely a scam, but they also thought it was an opportunity that could be potentially beneficial (BBC, n.d.). This shows that communication of winning something is hard to resist for some victims who go on to the next step of the fraud, which is to pay some amount to get the prize and part with some bank details. Scammers also show that they are part of governments or associated with big brands to con people into believing that their communications with them are genuine. They also put pressure on victims to act quickly to claim their prize.

Lottery email example(RUBENSTEIN, 2011):

From: Information Desk <info@euroonlinelottery.com>
Subject: EU / Commonwealth Lottery Promotions

Your email address was selected to claim the sum of $ 500,000.00 in the 2011 European lottery.
To claim your prize, please contact our agent in Lagos, Nigeria.
Contact person: [redacted]
Phone: [redacted]
Congratulations!

Source: https://securelist.com/congratulations-youve-won-the-reality-behind-online-lotteries/36450/

4. Technical Support Scams

An unsolicited call or pop-up message from technical support is often a recipe for disaster. The scammer—under the guise of providing technical support or installing a software update—requests the victim to provide access to their desktop. The scammer then goes on to install malware, which can give them access to files and control over the machine. Even if the number is local or looks legitimate, the best way to avoid this scam is to ignore the call or message, at least until the caller's credentials are verified.

5. Customer Care Scam: Double Trouble

Victims can fall into 'double trouble' by googling a customer care number that's fake. The victim—already in trouble because something has gone wrong, such as an undelivered parcel or a lost credit card—now lands in the hands of fraudsters instead of customer care agents. The fraudsters tactfully take all the sensitive personal information of the victim, which they aggregate and sell or use for their own nefarious plans of stealing money. In February 2023, The Business Insider India, citing XVigil's (CloudSEK's risk monitoring platform) Fake Customer Care module, reported that there are over 31,000 fake customer care numbers on the internet. The primary targets of these fraudsters are in the banking and finance entities (Pal. Anagh, 2023).

6. Phishing Scams

Phishing is the most common among all scams. Scammers have created thousands of variants of Phishing schemes using email and text messaging to trick you into giving them your personal and financial information. To protect oneself against phishing schemes, one must be very cautious in responding to emails, clicking on suspicious links, opening attachments and verifying if the sender of the email or message is in your contact list. Attachments and links could be used to install harmful malware. Using multi-factor authentication also provides another layer of protection even if a password is compromised.

Phishing statistics:

An estimated 3.4 billion phishing emails are sent every day. Stolen credentials are the most common cause of data breaches. Google alone blocks around 100 million phishing emails daily. More than 48 per cent of emails sent in 2022 were spam (Griffiths, 2023a, 2023b).

---

7. Vishing

Vishing is another form of phishing and refers to voice-based phishing. Here, scamsters use phone calls to deceive victims into sharing personal information, sending them money or giving them remote access to your computer. These take multiple forms, like Robocalls (automated calls), spoofed caller IDs and voicemails. Examples of Vishing calls are those where callers represent tax authorities, saying that "your bank account is compromised" or that your "insurance policy is being cancelled, unless....".

8. Email Fraud

Email is one of the prime vehicles for scamsters to perpetrate fraud. Just by using an email ID, they can call, threaten and harass individuals in multiple ways. They can ask or deceive an individual into clicking on links, downloading malware or impersonating someone important like a tax official, a family member, a friend, a colleague, a boss or a bank employee.

As an example of email spoofing, a scamster could create an email that looks like it comes from anyone other than himself. Contextually, such messages may warn a user that their account will be suspended if they do not click a link, authenticate into the site and set a new password.

Email fraud example:

Dear Microsoft User

This is the last time we notified you that we will stop processing incoming emails in your account reasons are you failed to verify your Microsoft account which may lead to permanent delete of your account from our data-base in the next few hours.

Kindly take a minute to complete our email verification below

Important Notice- Account disconnection will take place today 12:00 Midnight if issue not resolved.

Source:https://bccatholic.ca/voices/peter-vogel/email-based-scams-continue-unabated

9. Business Email Compromise

A business email compromise is a means or type of fraud where the scamster impersonates someone in authority to send money to an account controlled by him using fake contexts. Examples of BEC scams are covered earlier in this chapter. BEC scams use various props like fake invoices, lawyer impersonation, CEO/CFO impersonation, supplier bills, etc. BEC scams were on the rise when there was an increase in remote working necessitated due to the Covid-19 pandemic.

10. Imposter Scam

An imposter scam involves an email, call or text message where the scamster impersonates someone in authority to share your personal details so that they can use your ID information to commit fraud.

Example of imposter email: (Savvy Security, 2021)

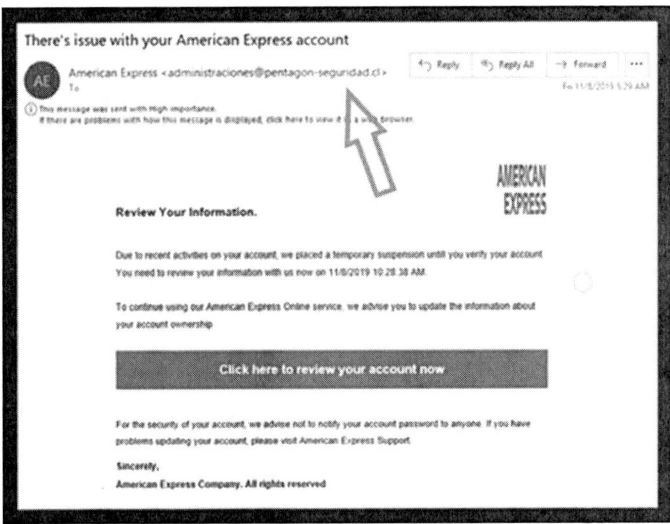

Source: https://cheapsslsecurity.com/blog/what-is-email-spoofing-an-explanation/

11. Charity and Disaster Fraud

Charity scams are often called the evil side of good. Charity scamsters typically ask for donations in person, on the phone, by email or through text messages for a cause that looks real or maybe even is a real cause or disaster that has taken place. The only difference here is that the money that you may remit will go into the coffers of the scamsters and not to the victims of a tragedy or unfortunate situation.

Example of a charity scam email (Bizga, 2023)

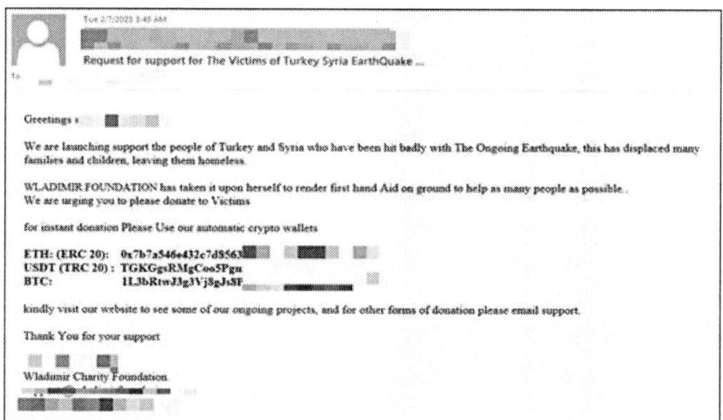

Tue 2/7/2023 3:48 AM

Request for support for The Victims of Turkey Syria EarthQuake ...

Greetings :

We are launching support the people of Turkey and Syria who have been hit badly with The Ongoing Earthquake, this has displaced many families and children, leaving them homeless

WLADIMIR FOUNDATION has taken it upon herself to render first hand Aid on ground to help as many people as possible .
We are urging you to please donate to Victims

for instant donation Please Use our automatic crypto wallets

ETH: (ERC 20): 0x7b7a546e432c7d8563
USDT (TRC 20) : TGKGgsRMgCoo5Pgn
BTC: 1L3bRtwJ3g3Vj8gJs8F

kindly visit our website to see some of our ongoing projects, and for other forms of donation please email support.

Thank You for your support

Wladimir Charity Foundation

Source: https://socradar.io/cybercriminals-seek-to-turn-humanitarian-crisis-into-opportunity/

12. Job Offer Scam

Scamsters put out fake job postings on popular websites and solicit applications. Knowing fully well that job applicants are vulnerable and eager to get the advertised job, they conduct fake interviews and even issue fake appointment letters. The catch here is that the prospective job applicant must pay a fee in advance to take care of administrative charges. A growing sub-segment of the job offers scam is the work-from-home job aspirants.

13. Cancellation Scam

Scamsters posing as delivery agents approach unsuspecting victims, stating that they have a package to deliver to them on a cash-on-delivery basis. When the victim says that they did not order for the same, the agent says that they will initiate an order cancellation process for which they require all your personal details, including an OTP (One Time Password). Using this OTP, the scamsters hack the cell phones of the victims and steal their money.

14. Healthcare Scams

The most common of healthcare scam is one where a scamster, posing as a health insurance salesman, attempts to deceive you into revealing personal information (name, address, social security number, credit card number, etc.).

During the recent COVID-19 pandemic, there were several fraudulent schemes where multiple communication modes, such as testing websites, telemarketing calls, text messages and social media platforms, were in play. Scamsters were offering illegitimate COVID-19 services in exchange for personal details.

15. Greeting Card Scam

All important occasions, at an individual level and at a societal level, are moments marked by celebrations. Greeting cards are often sent or exchanged on occasions such as birthdays, anniversaries, festivals, etc., via email. Hackers exploit this by installing malware into the greeting cards, which, when downloaded on the recipient's computer, can result in stealing information or personal data or using the computer as a bot.

16. Bank Loan Scam

Emails or messages offering loans on attractive and easy terms are something to watch out for. Scamsters entice you with offers like 'loan in minutes' or 'preapproved loans', drawing you into a discussion to avail of the loan. In the process, the scamsters seek your personal details and access to your mobile phone, leaving you completely compromised. When it comes to repayments, they make unreasonable demands and start harassing the victims and their families. There are hundreds of loan apps available on the internet, making it difficult to differentiate genuine ones from fake ones.

17. Credit Card Fraud

There is almost an endless stream of phone calls offering free credit cards. The agent claims that they represent a bank, and if you show any interest whatsoever, then they start asking you for your personal details. These scams continue to deceive people despite widespread awareness that such offers are too good to be true and should not be relied upon.

18. Investment Scams

An investment scam is one where innocent victims are enticed into handing over their money in the belief that they are making an investment. Such investment opportunities may be advertised online on social media and promise attractive returns. There is a closure date for making the investment, emphasising that if investments are not made by that date, then the opportunity no longer exists. Often, the investment opportunity is entirely fake, and the scamsters take all the invested money and disappear soon after. To hold your trust for a brief while, messages relating to the growth of your investments are sent to the victims so that they are lulled into a sense of security that their investments are safe.

19. Extortion Scams

Extortion emails are a type of scam where scamsters send threatening messages to individuals or organisations, demanding money in exchange for not releasing sensitive or embarrassing information.

Another common form of extortion is in the form of loan scams. The scamsters contact victims by calling them or by sending an SMS/email offering a loan. They introduce themselves as officers, representatives or agents of reputed banks or non-banking financial institutions. If the target victim is interested, the loan is quickly approved after a Know Your Customer (KYC), and the money is transferred to the victim. The scamsters trick users into agreeing to predatory loan contracts and ask them to grant access to sensitive information such as contacts and SMS messages. Their (the cybercriminals') objective is to exfiltrate excessive user data and harass victims into paying back huge amounts.

20. Sextortion Scams

A variation of extortion scams, here, photographs and videos (which may even be morphed) are used to demand payment for not releasing them or sharing them with the victim's family, friends, or contacts.

21. Identity Theft, AI-based Voice Cloning and Deep Fakes

Artificial Intelligence (AI) based voice cloning websites can clone voice samples with up to 99 per cent accuracy when compared to real human voices. Similarly, Deepfakes, which are the manipulation of facial appearance through deep generative methods, can be highly accurate and are designed to deceive. While the act of creating fake content is not new (hackers used Photoshopping earlier), deepfakes today leverage powerful techniques from machine learning and artificial intelligence to manipulate or generate visual and audio content that can be highly deceptive.

22. Life Insurance Scams

"Your insurance policy is expiring", say the callers. They go on to inform the potential victim that they can get a certain sum of money from a policy taken long ago from the insurance company that the callers represent. Due to the nonpayment of premiums, the policy is going to be cancelled, but there is a good amount of money that can accrue to the victim. The caller (scamster) then informs the victim that to get the 'surrender value' of the policy, they must pay an amount towards administration fees and processing charges. In reality, there is no insurance policy, and by the time the victim realises it, they have already parted with some money or personal information.

23. Crypto Scamming

The introduction of cryptocurrency has brought in a new wave of cybercrimes. It is used for all types of crimes that involve the transmission of monetary value. This includes Ponzi investment schemes, money laundering, financial sanctions evasions and other corruption-related crimes such as bribery and embezzlement.

Scamsters impersonate government officials of a nation-state and ask a victim to deposit money into a crypto wallet to escape from fraud charges. They provide fake technical support consultations to unsuspecting victims and coerce them into transferring funds in cryptocurrency. These ill-gotten cryptocurrency assets are subsequently routed through multiple crypto wallets, ultimately ending up in the perpetrators' crypto accounts (ANI, 2023).

An example of a cryptocurrency scam (Press Trust of India, 2023):

The Indian authorities arrested a Delhi resident who allegedly posed as a Canadian government official and coerced his targets into transferring their assets to crypto wallets before siphoning them off with his accomplices. The accused, Sahil Pal and Ashish Bhambani, were booked by the Central Bureau of Investigation (CBI) based on inputs from Canadian authorities. The duo allegedly posed as Canadian government officials and cheated Quebec-based Trishan Goussard. They asked Goussard to deposit CAD 7,006 (around INR 4.35 lakh) in a crypto wallet to avoid several fraud charges in his compromised social insurance number, the CBI has alleged (PTI, 2023a, 2023b).

24. Travel/Holiday Scams

The holiday season has become a season for cyber scams. Vacationers are anxious to make travel reservations, hotel bookings and other travel-related arrangements and look for attractive deals. Scamsters are well prepared for this every season and come up with deals that may even be too good to be true. Each year, thousands of people around the world become victims of holiday and other travel-related scams. The most prevalent form of holiday scam is where goods or services are not delivered even though they have been paid for. For vacationers, the shock hits them when they set off with family, friends and companions only to find that the arrangements they had so carefully made are not real, and the money paid has gone to hackers. It is best to ascertain and confirm the credentials of offers before proceeding with making bookings.

25. Government Agency Scams

Governments have a great influence on the daily lives of citizens. When citizens get phone calls or emails from scamsters pretending to be from a government agency, such as tax authorities or law enforcement agencies, they get scared that they may have committed some offence. The scamsters use this sense of fear to deceive victims into making payments to them, offering to save them from the trouble they are in.

Another type of government agency scam is where the scamsters offer access to government grants under various government schemes. They ask for an administrative fee with the promise that they will get these grants for them.

26. Investment-Cum-Part-Time-Job Fraud

Victims are lured by fraudsters in the name of investment-cum-part-time-jobs. They are asked to do simple tasks, such as liking YouTube videos or writing Google reviews, and are paid for completing them. The fraudsters encourage the victims to invest small amounts of up to Rs. 500, and they are initially given high returns, including double the money in some cases, after completing the first task. The investors are then asked to put in higher amounts in a series of 7-8 transactions. A fake window shows the money purportedly earned by the investors, but they are not allowed to withdraw the money till they complete all the tasks. By then, they have already put in thousands of dollars.

The Hyderabad (India) Police unearthed a mega fraud involving Chinese handlers, in which at least fifteen thousand Indians were swindled of over Rs. 700 crores in less than a year. According to the police, the money was transmitted to China via Dubai and some of it was also sent to an account operated by Hezbollah, the Lebanon-based terror group. Some part of the money was converted into cryptocurrency and deposited into a wallet operated by Hezbollah. In all, nine people were arrested, and the police are on the lookout for at least six more. As for the victims who were approached on Telegram and WhatsApp, they have lost Rs. 5-6 lakh on average (Sudhir, 2023).

27. Social Media Scams

Scamsters just love social media. It helps them gather valuable information about potential target victims and also gives them insights into their interests and preferences. Scamsters can also create alternate personalities on social media by using someone else's name, photos, and other identifying information. Using these fake accounts, scamsters can request money, send links to download malware and make friends with potential victims. In fact, scamsters have also started impersonating celebrities.

Among the various types of social media scams, romantic scams comprise almost one-fourth of all social media scams. A typical romantic scam starts with befriending a target person (carefully selected based on social media profile) using an attractive social profile, such as a wealthy doctor or space researcher. Once the initial friendship is established through intense interaction on social media, promises are made of marriage and settling down. Then suddenly, a message is received that the scamster is stuck in a difficult situation and needs money to get out of it. Since the trust is established, the victim makes the payment. More payments are asked for and even made under one pretext or the other until the victim realises that they have been conned.

Georgina, a widow, took to Facebook to stay connected with family and friends. One day, she received a friend request from Jim, who was a stranger working for the military in an overseas assignment. Overtime, they became friendly. It all started with Jim sharing with her that he had some legal issues and needed money to get home. Georgina sent more than USD 100,000 before her family and the police found out that Jim was just a scamster (Masjedi, 2023).

28. Car Insurance Scam

A lawyer, Nitin Soni, who ironically deals with cases of cyber fraud, became a victim himself when a lady caller, posing as a representative of a leading online insurance broker, sold him a fake car insurance policy at an attractive rate (PTI, 2023a, 2023b).

This is a common scam wherein the scamster is aware of the previous policy details and the expiry date. Car owners would like to renew the policy before the expiry date for multiple reasons, including the fact that they must go through an elaborate car inspection exercise if they do not renew before the due date. Using a company logo that represents a popular insurance broking company is all that is needed for the scamster to establish legitimacy. Once done, the insurance premium is paid, and a fake receipt is issued. The car owner is under the impression that he has renewed his car insurance until an untoward incident involving the car happens, and the fraud is discovered. In this case, the lawyer realised the fraud a few days later when he spotted a spelling error in his name in the policy document and reached out to the insurance company to get it corrected (O'Neill, 2023).

29. SIM Swapping and SIM Cloning Frauds

A Subscriber Identity Module (SIM) card is a small card that contains a chip which fits into a smartphone and is essential for your smartphone to work. It enables you to make or receive calls and send texts. The SIM card in your phone also holds plenty of information, such as user identity, location and phone number, network authorisation data, personal security keys, contact lists and stored text messages.

In a SIM swap scam, cybercriminals take control of a victim's phone by stealing their SIM card and inserting it into another phone. Once this is done, they have access to all the data that is stored and save it on the cloud. Bank accounts can also be accessed as transaction OTPs are sent to the mobile phone. Once scamsters take control of a victim's phone, they can perform various types of potentially harmful cybercrimes.

In one of the most high-profile cases of SIM swapping, fraudsters managed to gain control over Twitter CEO Jack Dorsey's phone number and went on to seize control of his Twitter handle for a full 15 minutes.

The SIM Collector

31-year-old Nasim Malitya, a resident of Heropara village in Kashipur town, located in Murshidabad, West Bengal, ran an unusual business. He made a business of supplying active mobile connections and pre-activated user accounts to scamsters. His village was a hub for scrap business, particularly of old mobile phones. Malitya found an opportunity in removing the SIM cards from discarded devices. He then identified the active SIM cards from the rest and sold them to scamsters. Malitya also provided value-added services by offering one-time passwords for scamsters to register on platforms like WhatsApp and e-commerce websites such as OLX, where scams often happen. He side-stepped know-your-customer (KYC) processes and used SIM cards registered under genuine names of unsuspecting individuals. When he was arrested, the police found a staggering 21,761 pre-activated SIM cards stored in his house. It is noteworthy that his operations were not limited to India but also covered countries like the United Arab Emirates, Bangladesh, Sri Lanka, Bhutan and Nepal (Singh, 2023).

Recognising the rising cases of SIM fraud in India, the government of India has revised the rules for the issue and verification of SIM cards. According to the new rules, all SIM card dealers will have to complete police and biometric verification with mandatory registration. The issuance of bulk connections has also been discontinued. More than 52 lakh connections obtained using fraudulent methods have been deactivated and over 67,000 dealers have been blacklisted (India News, 2023).

30. Celebrity Scams

The scamster here pretends to be a celebrity in order to obtain personal information, including credit card numbers, bank account information and passwords, from unsuspecting victims, who often let their guard down when they think they are dealing with famous people. Scamsters here use social media, fake websites and emails to lure people into believing and trusting them. There are various flavours of celebrity scams, right from asking fans to contribute to a charity (fake) or make an investment that will fetch them good returns (again fake). Out of a sense of loyalty, many fans do as they are told and lose money.

31. Free/Discounted Products and Services

It is hard to resist the temptation of buying a product or service when it is offered at a heavily discounted price. Scamsters use this to their advantage by offering well-known brands through dodgy websites at unbelievable prices to tempt you to place an order and make a payment. Their goal is to take your money and not deliver the ordered item.

32. Fine Print Scams

The internet is full of offers that seem too good to be true. For example, there are advertisements for weight loss products which offer free trials as well as those offering a full refund if the product is not to the consumer's satisfaction. There is, however, a fine print in the user agreement that provides the fraudsters with escape clauses for not refunding any amount.

33. Electricity Bill Payment Scam

The electric bill payment scam has all the elements that are favourable for the scamster. Every random consumer has a phone number, where a simple SMS is required to be sent. A typical SMS reads, "Dear Consumer, your electricity will be disconnected tonight since there is an outstanding bill amount of Rs. XXX to be paid. To avoid disconnection, please click on the following link to pay the bill." Other elements, such as a definitive amount which needs to be paid, a due date (often immediate) to drive home the sense of urgency, a credible reason to make the payment (for electricity supplies) and a payment link which ensures that the payment (if made) goes directly to the scamsters account are reliable markers of these kinds of scams.

34. Fake Antivirus Software

There are multiple types of fake apps. Among the most dangerous of them are fake antivirus apps. Before buying antivirus software, people search for apps that meet their requirements. Cybercriminals have become adept at creating fake apps of various types, which, when downloaded, run scans and show the presence of a (fake) virus on the victim's computer. The same is communicated through a pop-up message to the victim, who is now worried about the data on their computer. The cybercriminals demand money to clean up the victim's computer and make it free from the (fake) virus. If the app notifications that their phone or computer is infected do not scare the target victims, the app will keep running in the background and spy on them using the webcam and microphone, and maybe even logging every key that they press.

35. Account Failure/Problem

One of the most common messages that you can find in your spam folder are supposedly from your email services provider informing you that your account needs to be validated by entering your password, failing which the account may get deactivated. Sometimes, these messages also land in your inbox, asking you to take action if you don't want to risk the deactivation of your account. The objective of this kind of email is to make you fill out a form that looks genuine, wherein you are asked to enter your active password and provide other login details like your username. Once the scamster has gained access to the account in question using the stolen login credentials, they can change the password and seize control over the account such that the legitimate user can no longer access it.

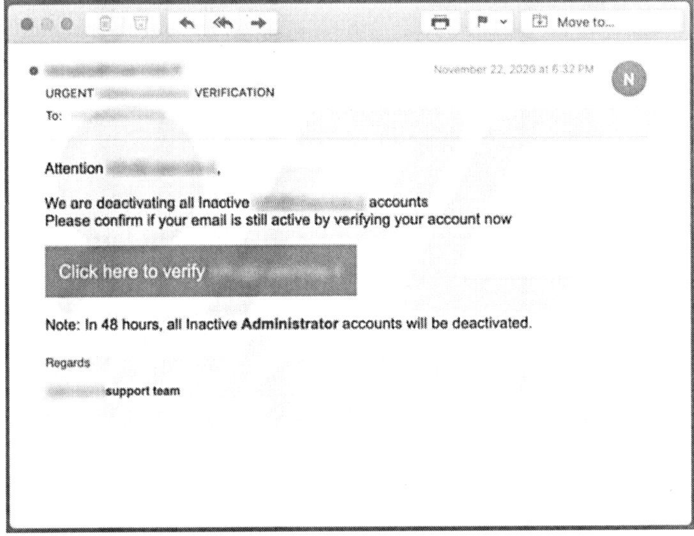

Source: https://www.pcrisk.com/removal-guides/19488-deactivating-all-inactive-accounts-email-scam

35. Fake Websites

An elaborate way for scamsters to lure people into giving up their personal details, including login credentials and credit card information, is through the use of mirror websites. These websites are identical to the website of a big bank or e-commerce store, with the exception that there is a small change in the website domain name. The website looks and functions like the original website but is designed to only capture user information.

36. Ticket Scams

A big event of interest is announced, and everyone is waiting for the tickets to be available. The scamster sees this as an opportunity to create a ticket-selling website online and get people to pay for tickets that they will never get or are fake. Even when events are sold out, these fake websites sell (fake) tickets at exorbitant prices and make money. In their eagerness to grab tickets, fans often do not exercise caution and get duped.

37. Tax Refund Scam

For this type of scam, scamsters call individuals or send them a SMS to urge them to update personal and bank information on an attached link so that their tax refund can be processed. Many people who fall for this soon find their accounts drained of funds.

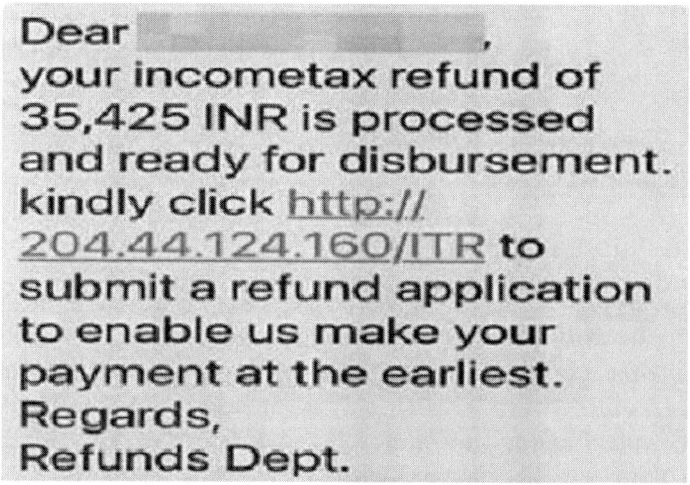

Dear ,
your incometax refund of 35,425 INR is processed and ready for disbursement. kindly click http://204.44.124.160/ITR to submit a refund application to enable us make your payment at the earliest.
Regards,
Refunds Dept.

Source: https://www.moneylife.in/article/beware-sms-for-income-tax-refund-with-links-is-fraud-users-are-lured-to-fake-sites-of-i-t-dept-sbi-icici-bank-axis-bank-pnb-and-hdfc-bank/63218.html

39. Hitman Scam

For a victim, being caught in this kind of scam is a big nightmare. An email or SMS informs the victim that the sender has received a contract for killing them. The so-called 'hitman' demands a certain sum of money (typically between USD 1000 and USD 100,000) to spare the life of the potential victim. The sender also issues a warning that their associates are watching the victim's movements and that they (the victim) should not report the SMS or email to the police (Government of Western Australia, n.d.).

40. Coupon Scam

In October 2021, the New York Post reported on what could be called "the mother of all coupon scams". Lori Ann Talens, from Virginia Beach (Virginia, USA), had a special talent for creating bogus coupons and swindled retailers out of USD 32 million. Talens utilised her marketing and computer design skills to create fake coupons for nearly 13,000 products. When she was arrested, the law enforcement authorities seized designs on her computer as well as more than USD 1 million worth of phony coupons. She was able to counterfeit coupons for virtually any grocery or drug store product and make it for whatever value she wanted. She was sentenced to a 12-year prison term (O'Neill, 2021).

41. 'Rug-Pull' Crypto Scams

Cryptocurrencies are attracting a lot of attention all over the world from an alternative investment point of view. The opportunity to earn higher returns than other investment forms lures investors to buy cryptocurrencies, making them vulnerable to cybersecurity scams. The 'Rug-pull' is a kind of scam that happens when a project is hyped up through marketing efforts, which results in big investment flows. As the traction is still there, scamsters literally pull the rug from under the feet of investors and stop all withdrawals (Dirchi, 2023).

42. Student Loan Scholarships/Grants

Students often look for scholarships and loan waivers to reduce the burden of their education on their parents and others who support them. Scamsters prey on educational loan borrowers, promising loan waivers or scholarships. Under this pretext, they ask the student to pay a fee for their help.

Example of student loan forgiveness mail (Skope, 2015).

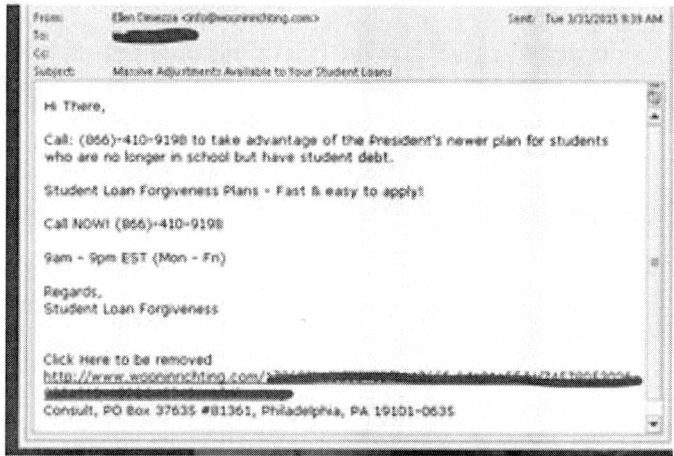

From: [illegible] Sent: [illegible]
To:
Cc:
Subject: Massive Adjustments Available to Your Student Loans

Hi There,

Call: (866)-410-9198 to take advantage of the President's newer plan for students who are no longer in school but have student debt.

Student Loan Forgiveness Plans - Fast & easy to apply!

Call NOW! (866)-410-9198

9am - 9pm EST (Mon - Fri)

Regards,
Student Loan Forgiveness

Click Here to be removed
[illegible]
Consult, PO Box 37635 #81361, Philadelphia, PA 19101-0635

Source: https://skopemag.com/2015/04/07/beware-student-loan-forgiveness-scams

43. Software Sales Scam

Kolkata has become a hub for this type of scam. Scamsters make calls to Western English-speaking countries seeking to sell a product from Microsoft, Amazon or Norton malware software. The next step is to get the potential victim to click on a link or confuse them with an error. They then seek access to install a remote desktop software like TeamViewer or AnyDesk, which gives the scamster complete control over the victim's computer (Menon, 2022).

44. Pharming

Pharming is a scam wherein scamsters redirect the traffic from a genuine website to a lookalike fake website, especially e-commerce or banking sites. Pharming is associated with harvesting login credentials on a large-scale and is also referred to as "phishing without a lure"(Proofpoint, n.d.). Scamsters create counterfeit websites that closely resemble genuine ones to deceive unsuspecting users into revealing their personal information, such as usernames, passwords, credit card details, or other sensitive data. When users type in the address of any website, they expect to be directed to the genuine one, but the pharming code that is running on the victim's computer redirects them to a fake version. It does not require clicking on a link and, hence, is more potent than some other forms of phishing.

45. Courier Fraud

Courier scams are on the rise, especially in India. Scamsters make a call, impersonating executives from a courier company to inform victims that a parcel containing illegal items has been seized by customs authorities. The victim then gets a call from people claiming to be officers from the Central Bureau of Investigation (CBI), asking the victims to make a payment to a designated account to prevent them from being implicated in the crime. A student from Bengaluru was made to pay Rs 134,650 after falling for such a courier scam (Bhati, 2023a, 2023b).

46. Typosquatting

Typosquatting is a form of cybersquatting, where scamsters own domain names similar to popular brand names, such that people who incorrectly enter the wrong Uniform Resource Locator (URL)—for example, they enter 'Amazzon.com' instead of Amazon.com'—they land up on the scamsters fake website and end up compromising their credentials and even credit card information.

48. Pension/Fake Provident Fund (PF) Payout Scam

Pension scams are targeted towards the immediate cash needs of pensioners. Scamsters posing as representatives of pension funds try to lure a victim with special one-time offers which can help them get higher upfront cash than their current schemes allow. They also propose other deals with higher guaranteed returns. The scamsters will try to convince the victim that to do this, they need to transfer the redeemed pension funds to them for reinvestment, with the fake promise of high returns.

According to a report on News18 website, an elderly couple in Mumbai was defrauded of Rs 4.35 crores by callers claiming to be from the Employee Provident Fund Organisation. The callers told them that they were entitled to get Rs 11 crores from a corpus accrued from past savings. They persuaded the couple pay Rs 4.35 crores to their accounts stating that Tax Deducted at Source (TDS), Goods and Services Tax (GST) and income tax had to be paid in advance. It was only when the callers kept demanding more money that the couple realize that they had been duped.

Source:https://www.news18.com/business/provident-fund-payout-pf-scam-mumbai-news-8634798.html

49. Bank Impersonator Racket (KYC Scams)

Know Your Customer (KYC) is a very important part of the financial world. Regulatory bodies insist that banks and financial services organisations update their KYC data on an annual basis. Banks, in turn, call or email their customers to update their KYC information. Scamsters use this context to call a customer posing as banking officials and ask them to share their details to update KYC. They threaten them that in case they do not do so, their accounts will be blocked. The most common KYC scams involve the use of fake or duplicate KYC, Phishing, identity theft and Smishing (a variant of phishing using SMS).

50. 'Likes' Scam

It sounds incredible, but a man received Rs 150 after liking YouTube videos and ended up losing Rs 40 lakh in the online scam. This work-from-home scam involves watching YouTube videos and posting 'likes' on them. A man from Ahmedabad fell for this trick when he was offered money for posting likes. He was paid small sums of Rs 50 for the likes he posted, which was shown as a credit balance in an account statement purportedly to show his earnings. He was added to a Telegram group comprising over 50 persons where everyone was happy to make easy money. After completing some basic video-liking tasks, he was offered other tasks where he could make more money. For receiving these tasks, he was asked to make some prepaid amounts and was added to more Telegram groups. Before he realised that he was being duped, he had already made payments amounting to Rs. 40 lakhs (Bhati, 2023a, 2023b).

We have just examined fifty different types of scams. Each of these scams has their own variants. Scamsters are also continuously innovating and adding to their repertoire of committing fraud. When it comes to cyberattacks, installing firewalls, antivirus software and other cybersecurity solutions can enhance our security to a great extent. However, when it comes to defending ourselves against scams, it is much more difficult. Scams play on the human psyche, which can be manipulated or exploited into taking actions that could jeopardise security due to ignorance, a lack of knowledge, greed, fear, vanity, lust, and any number of human weaknesses.

Avoiding online scams requires a number of actions to be taken, with the most important among them being the ability to recognise a scam when confronted with one. Surviving in the digital world requires developing one's awareness of scams, being vigilant when online and being diligent when it comes to taking online actions. Here is a list of tips that can help you in staying safe. There are no guarantees here, and each person must constantly strive to protect themselves while navigating the online world.

- If you receive any offer online that is too good to be true, it probably is. Stay clear of such offers.
- Always verify the contact information of the sender before responding or taking any actions.
- Do not visit dubious websites and click on pop-ups or suspicious links.
- Do not give away your personal or financial information in response to a request that you did not expect. Safeguard your personal information, credit card numbers, OTPs, etc., always.
- Use all basic cybersecurity protections like firewalls, antivirus software and Virtual Private Networks (VPNs), and avoid using Public Wi-Fi Systems.
- Safeguard your mobile phone and other devices by setting software to update automatically.
- Guard your accounts by using multi-factor authentication.
- Protect your data by backing it up.
- Block all unwanted callers and messages.
- Do not get pressured into urgent actions. Think, check, verify and then act. Another way is to stop and talk to someone you can trust before you take any action.

With the increasing role that the internet plays in our daily lives, we are at a much greater risk of becoming a victim of online scams than ever before. While the above steps are a useful means of protection from online scams, we need to constantly update ourselves with regard to new forms of online scams to stay safe. While internet scams have no boundaries, there are countries that have become hubs of cyber scam activities.

According to Analytics Insight, the following are the top 10 internet-scamming countries in the world in 2023 (Akash, 2023a):

The top 10 internet scamming countries in the world in 2023 (Akash, 2023b)

1. Nigeria	6. Romania
2. Ghana	7. Russia
3. India	8. South Africa
4. Indonesia	9. Ukraine
5. Philippines	10. United States

If one is an unfortunate victim of a cyber scam or has even been targeted by a scam, it is in the best interests of the person concerned that they inform or file a formal report with law enforcement authorities, which are dedicated to detecting as well as preventing cyber scams and frauds. Not only can this action save you from being scammed further, but the authorities can also use the information to build cases against scamsters, identify new types of scams, spot trends and educate the public to beware of such scams.

11

Future Shock

Cyberattacks of the future will leverage new technologies, be deadlier, more sophisticated and multifaceted. Their ability to cause harm could be unprecedented, and greater all-round efforts will be required to avert them or minimise the damage caused by them.

As technologies continue to evolve and grow, damage from cyberattacks has also shown a dramatic increase. Experts estimate that cyberattacks will cause damage worth about USD 10.5 trillion annually by 2025, which represents a 300 per cent increase from 2010 levels (Douthwaite, 2022). This shows that cybercriminals are highly motivated to stay ahead of the latest security trends. They are also faster and smarter than most people in leveraging new technologies for malicious purposes and have shown the ability to launch more sophisticated and devastating attacks. Unfortunately for us, cybercrime is growing faster than our ability to defend ourselves.

Alvin Toffler was an American futurist and author whose book *Future Shock* was published in 1970. He co-wrote it with his wife, Adelaide Farrell, on how modern technologies, including the digital revolution and the communication revolution, would impact cultures worldwide. The authors defined the term "future shock" as "the shattering stress and disorientation that we induce in individuals by subjecting them to too much change in too short a time. Change is not merely necessary to life—it is life. Technology feeds on itself"(Model Thinkers, n.d.). Even as the rapid speed of technological change induces its own element of shock in our lives, there is also the shock that comes from sudden and adverse cyber events such as cyberattacks and cybercrimes. In this context, here is a definition of Cyber Shock: a state of disbelief, anxiety and panic that arises from receiving the news or discovering that you (an individual or organisation) have been the target/victim of a cyberattack, data breach or online scam.

2023 will be remembered as the start of a new generation of AI applications. ChatGPT, which heralded this new revolution, reached a million users faster than any other application. OpenAI's ChatGPT, which is a text-generating AI chatbot, has taken the world by storm with its potential uses for answering questions, composing emails, essays and even writing code.

A World Economic Forum survey in 2017, as a part of their Technology Tipping Points and Societal Impact report, predicted the following:

Technology tipping points expected to occur by 2025

- Ten per cent of people will be wearing clothes connected to the Internet
- There will be the first robotic pharmacist in the US
- The first 3-D car will be in production
- Ninety per cent of the population will have regular access to the internet
- Driverless cars will be equal to about ten per cent of all cars on US roads
- The first transplant of a 3-D liver will happen
- Over fifty per cent of internet traffic will be to homes for appliances and devices
- We will see the world's first city of more than fifty thousand with no traffic lights
- There will be the first AI-powered machine on a corporate board of directors

Source: World Economic Forum

When it comes to technology, it seems as though the future is rushing at us. Predicting the future of information, computers and telecommunication technologies can be quite daunting.

Technologies are evolving at a furious pace, and before we realise it, they become a part of our daily lives, and what is more, we become completely dependent on them. This makes it difficult for cybersecurity personnel and experts to prepare for what is to come. Hackers are quick to identify opportunities in this fast-moving technology landscape and gain an upper hand over the defenders.

To identify future cyber shocks that we could be subjected to, we need to examine the following key technology trends that, while providing great benefits, will also enable cyberattacks that are bigger in scale, in sophistication and in terms of the potential damage that they can cause.

1. Everything on the Internet

According to an article in Security Intelligence, an award-winning thought leadership blog run by IBM Security, by the year 2030, the "Internet of Things" age will be over, and we will reach the "Everything is Internet" age (Platsis, 2023).

Futurists believe that by 2030, connectivity will have a bearing on every aspect of daily life. We are already moving from an IoT era to an era of the Internet of Everything (IoE). In several ways, IoE is an extension of IoT. IoE is a superset of IoT that encompasses five key elements: network, things or objects, people, data and processes that provide general intelligence and improved cognition across the networked ecosystem. IoE is a unified system that enhances the capabilities of the connected entities and brings in network intelligence to enable smarter decision-making and easy data exchange.

In an IoE environment, any object, appliance or activity can be equipped with digital features. It can thus create a distributed ecosystem capable of generating valuable data and automatically turning it into actions for businesses, industries and individuals.

Imagine the next generation of smart cities, where every aspect of the environmental, economic and social aspects of urban life, including basic aspects like housing, transportation, energy systems and infrastructure, are all a part of an IoE ecosystem. By 2030, the number of electric vehicles, vans, heavy trucks and buses on the road worldwide is estimated to reach 145 million (Huawei, 2023). While this will make citizens' lives easier, it will also provide malicious threat actors an opportunity to use and abuse technological innovation, just as they have always done.

When we examine the future of technology, perhaps one of the strongest influences has been science fiction. Science fiction draws inspiration for solving real-world problems, which in turn spurs innovation and creates technologies from cell phones to virtual reality, and from smart homes to smart cities with connected cars and autonomously flying drones, new shopping experiences and working and socialising in the metaverse. This means that there will be sensors everywhere.

There are differing estimates about the number of IoT devices among experts as shown below:

The number of Internet of Things (IoT) devices worldwide is estimated to nearly double from 15.1 billion in 2020, to more than 29 billion IoT devices in 2030 (Vailshery, 2023).
International Data Corporation (IDC) estimates that there will be 41.6 billion IoT devices in 2025 (IDC, 2021).
It is estimated that there will be more than 75 billion IoT-connected devices in use by 2025, a nearly threefold increase from 2019 figures (Statista, 2016).
Frost & Sullivan says that over the next 8 years, the earth will have a complex network of 200 billion devices, averaging over 20 connected devices per human (Frost & Sullivan, 2020)

Whatever the exact number of devices, we can be sure that we are headed towards a complex environment of a very large number of interconnected devices that promises us the convenience of automation along with enhancements in efficiency and productivity. We are in the midst of a frantic race to automate everything that we can by introducing new smart devices in every sphere of activity, along with providing enhanced bandwidth and computing power. But is all this coming at the cost of sacrificing cybersecurity?

The explosion in the number of IoT devices represents a greater opportunity for launching DDoS attacks. In general, IoT devices have had a poor track record when it comes to in-built security, making them vulnerable to being used as bots in order to generate fake traffic. Hackers today have the tools and malware needed to create vast botnets and generate traffic volumes running to terabytes per second.

The famous Spamhaus (an anti-spam service) attack in 2013 generated fake traffic at a rate of 300 gigabits per second (Gbps) (Vijayan, 2013). In 2016, a DDoS attack on a single customer of OVH, a French cloud computing company, involved an estimated 145,000 bots generating a traffic load of up to 1.1 terabits per second. The DDoS attack lasted about seven days (Nicholson, 2022).

Four years later, in 2020, Amazon Web Services was the target of a massive DDoS attack, which, at its peak, saw traffic at a rate of 2.3 terabits per second (Tbps) (Nicholson, 2022). In 2021, the scale of these attacks created new records. In November 2021, Microsoft suffered a DDoS attack targeting an Azure customer, which had a throughput of 3.45 Tbps and a packet rate of 340 million packets per second. This is believed to be the largest DDoS attack ever recorded (Lakshmanan, 2022).

In the future, we could see massive DDoS attacks which utilise the increased bandwidth offered by 5G and 6G, which could involve gigantic botnets comprising millions of bots and generate massive DDoS floods running into Peta bits per second, or even Exa bits per second, which can paralyse giants like Google or Amazon, smart city networks or even big sections of the internet for days.

2. 5G and 6G Greater Bandwidth, Bigger Attack Surface, More Vulnerabilities

Even as 5G rollouts are happening all over the world, technology researchers are already getting ready with 6G. Factors like speed, low latency, high reliability, bandwidth-hungry applications and more powerful online user experience are driving forces as wireless communication becomes a bigger part of our daily lives.

Using 5G, we can download an entire movie in less than a minute, while 6G promises that we can download more than 140 hours of movies in that same minute.

Source:https://www.6gworld.com/exclusives/guest-editorial-the-future-of-a-6g-enabled-world/

The rollout of 6G is expected to happen around 2030, which will coincide with the massive growth in IoT devices, the advent of quantum computing, the Yottabyte era, the next wave of AI and ML, and more. All this will herald a new era with enormous possibilities. However, security will remain a top concern as so many new technologies will each come with their own vulnerabilities, which will provide great opportunities for hackers.

5G vs. 6G: A Massive Leap in Power

6G will operate on terahertz (THz) bands from 100GHz to 10THz and deliver a peak data rate of 1000 gigabits/second with an air latency lower than 100 microseconds. In effect, 6G will be 50 times faster than 5G, 100 times more reliable, offer wider coverage and support ten times more devices per square kilometre.

When compared to 4G, 5G offers low latency under 5 milliseconds (ms), while 4G latency ranges from 60ms to 98ms. 4G offers download speeds of up to 1 Gbps, while 5G can go up to maximum download speeds of 10 Gbps. 6G networks promise to deliver speeds of 1 terabyte/second.

One of the biggest differences between 4G and its successor networks (5G and 6G networks) is the virtualisation of network functions previously performed by hardware. While this change in approach enables better management, monitoring and optimisation of networks, it also makes them more susceptible to attacks. If hackers gain control of the software that manages the networks, they can identify and exploit vulnerabilities in several ways, ranging from wrongful access to malware and DDoS attacks.

In a digital world powered by 6G, we can imagine global companies, along with their supply chains, manufacturing systems and consumers, all seamlessly connected, with every activity, from order placement to delivery, being fully automated.

6G will also enable everything to be connected (IoE) between cyber and physical systems. Furthermore, companies will work completely online, with meetings and video conferencing in the Metaverse. The Metaverse promises to bring new levels of social connection, mobility and collaboration to a 3-D world of virtual work through 'avatars' representing real people and immersive technologies such as virtual reality and augmented reality headsets.

In such a scenario, 5G and 6G networks will have a significantly larger attack surface than their predecessors, thanks to innovations in IoE, virtualised networks and open-source technologies. The biggest challenge will be security since the software-defined foundation of 5G and 6G brings about various new security concerns that could lead to theft of sensitive data, disruptions of connected devices and attacks on the network itself at an unprecedented scale (Hattar, 2021).

Malicious threat actors will evolve to use and leverage the power of 5G and 6G networks and exploit vulnerabilities to their advantage. As the use of AI and ML gets more widespread in building autonomous networks, hackers, too, will have to up their game and develop skills that are required to exploit the technology for their purposes.

Major cyberattacks in the era of 6G will depend on the ability of threat actors to manipulate machine learning models during training or testing times. It will also be possible for hackers to reverse engineer algorithms to extract proprietary information. As 6G networks will be designed to operate in an autonomous, self-preserving way that can respond independently to potential threats without causing disruption to normal use, AI will be required to play a key role in investigating adversarial machine learning approaches to train models to identify probable threats and determine an appropriate correlating response (Accesswire, 2022).

A completely smart city paralysed by the forces of evil (hackers) demanding a ransom to restore services seems to be straight out of a science fiction movie. Given the large number of cases of cities and public infrastructure being compromised by ransomware in recent times, this future scenario is not hard to imagine. Urban infrastructure, including emergency services, transport, traffic light management, healthcare, CCTV, power, water supply systems, and more, are increasingly becoming connected to 5G Internet of Things (IoT) services and sensors to collect data that can be used to provide better, more efficient services. The chaos and panic caused by such an attack that disrupts all essential services across a city of millions of people will be nothing short of catastrophic.

3. From Terabytes to Yottabytes

With increasing connectivity and more applications and devices generating real-time data, global data volumes have been growing continuously. According to a study by market researcher IDC, the global volume of data will be around 570 zettabytes in the year 2030, which is ten times greater than it was in 2020 (IDC, 2020). According to a study by Huawei, the Chinese multinational technology company, data generated worldwide every year by 2030 would be one Yottabyte, which would mean a 23-fold increase compared to 2020 (Huawei, 2023).

1024 gigabytes make a terabyte, 1024 terabytes make a petabyte, an exabyte consists of 1024 petabytes, a zettabyte consists of 1024 exabytes, and a yottabyte counts 1024 zettabytes.

Such high volumes of data will also include massive amounts of behavioural data of individuals. Data from various aspects of human life collected from wearables (health data), office computers, entertainment systems to movements (travel information), asset ownership (from smart buildings, cars), etc., as well as their other interests, will be stored and analysed. This will lead to accurate and unique behavioural profiling of each user. By gaining unauthorised access to such detailed profiles, hackers can launch sophisticated social engineering attacks exploiting vulnerabilities in smart devices and a lack of end-user awareness. These attacks will compel end-users, law enforcement and governments alike to find new ways to prevent social engineering and improve authentication (ENISA, 2023).

Another cyber threat scenario that can be envisioned is one that plays out in outer space. Governments and societies all over the world are increasingly dependent on satellites, and organised hacking groups could target them to gain control of these satellites that are owned by both public and private agencies. These skilled hackers could gain initial access via supply chain attacks on partners of satellite infrastructure organisations. They would then establish and maintain their presence in the space infrastructure, including base stations. Base stations are transceivers that connect satellites to a central terrestrial hub that, in turn, connects the satellite to a network. Having these key elements of space infrastructure under their control, hackers will use available techniques to remain undetected while launching DDoS and other types of attacks onto the target and disrupt critical military and civilian systems. The introduction of space-based cyber weapons may create shock waves in the world and even bring about changes in the geopolitical power equations (ENISA, 2023).

4. Cyber Weapons and Polymorphic Malware

Weaponised malware is a new and emerging threat that can be used to attack, disrupt or sabotage computer systems, networks or devices. Cyber weapons are designed for carrying out specific tasks such as reconnaissance, espionage, stealing data, destroying hardware, manipulating information or causing physical damage. The creation and evolution of cyber weapons pose a serious challenge to security and defence in the next few decades.

Cyber weapons of the future will be designed using building blocks from technologies such as quantum computing, advanced AI and ML and polymorphic malware. Polymorphic malware refers to a type of malware that constantly changes its characteristics in order to evade detection. It comprises a mutation engine with code that has the ability to morph and self-propagate. It also uses an encryption key to change its shape and signature. It combines a mutation engine with self-propagating code to current forms of polymorphic malware that exist in various forms, such as viruses and bots. VRLOCK,

URSNIF, VOBFUS and BAGLE are some of the most notorious polymorphic viruses in existence. Used in tandem with other malicious routines, polymorphic malware poses a great risk to its victims.

Using present-day AI tools like ChatGPT, hackers can generate dynamic, mutating versions of malicious code at each call, making the resulting vulnerability exploits difficult to detect by cybersecurity tools. By incorporating more and newer AI strains into malware code, polymorphic malware can become increasingly hard to detect while it continues to work towards meeting its deployment objectives. Polymorphic malware code would be fully context-aware, able to change both tactics and behaviour in response to—or even to anticipate—a security mechanism or state to its advantage.

Future generations of polymorphic malware will take the form of purpose-driven cyber weapons which can generate dynamic, mutating, malicious code, making it difficult for cybersecurity tools of the day to detect and defend against. It is more than likely that in the future, large-scale cyberattacks can be carried out using polymorphic malware. Such attacks will be hard to block because of the changing nature of the malware, even once it is inside a target network. This means that a single successful phishing email could morph into an attack that quickly moves through an entire network, exfiltrating data and utilising resources for crypto mining or even bringing entire systems to a halt (Johnson, 2020).

Autonomous cyber weapons will be used not only for military purposes but for cybercrime in general. It is quite frightening to imagine a cyber weapon in action that leverages extreme computing power to unleash algorithms working at superhuman speeds that can cause large-scale damage or catastrophic accidents. Similarly, cybercrimes against individuals can be carried out by robots that can conduct real-time impersonation of both systems and people, leading to dangerous consequences.

5. Quantum Computing

The cyber-world is waiting with bated breath for the advent of quantum computing. The exponential processing capability of a quantum computer is expected to drive revolutionary changes in the cyber landscape. While there is consensus among experts that, at present, quantum computers are in a lab or proof-of-concept stage, there are some who believe that several large organisations will undertake initiatives revolving around quantum computing as early as 2025. Most believe that it would take over a decade for its commercial use and deployment (Meige, 2023).

The race to build the most powerful quantum computer is on. Internet giants Alphabet Inc. (Google), Microsoft, Amazon and IBM are some of the big names that are playing an important role in advancing quantum computing hardware and software.

In 2019, Google announced it has a quantum computer that is 100 million times faster than any classical computer in its lab.

The cyber world is increasingly and ceaselessly generating data (we produce 2.5 exabytes of data every day). This is the equivalent of content on 5 million laptops. Moving forward, in the future, only quantum computers will make it possible to process the amount of data we are generating in the age of 'big data'.

IBM announced the Eagle, a 127 qubits processor, claiming it was the most powerful quantum processor in the world in 2021, surpassing China's 113-qubit Jiuzhang 2.0, Google's 72-qubit Bristlecone and IBM's own 65-qubit Hummingbird processor.

IBM intends to scale up its quantum computer to over 4,000 qubits by 2025 and beyond (Irving, 2021).

As per McKinsey's estimation, by 2030, the number of operational quantum computers is expected to reach approximately five thousand (Zaheer, 2023).

Just as with most new technologies, there are also security concerns that surround quantum computing. The biggest among them is related to its ability to decrypt data that uses present-day encryption algorithms. Currently, data in the world is protected using asymmetric cryptography algorithms such as Rivest–Shamir–Adleman (RSA), Diffie-Hellman (DH) and Elliptic Curve Cryptography (ECC). Quantum computing will be able to crack these algorithms quite easily, rendering the current asymmetric encryption methods unsafe.

Realising that at some future date they may be able to gain access to the power of quantum computers, hackers have devised a new methodology known as 'harvest now, decrypt later' (HNDL). HNDL attacks pose a major threat to data-rich organisations such as banks, financial institutions, intelligence agencies, militaries and large corporations. This puts all sensitive personal information, confidential information of corporates and governments (that is considered secure today as it exists in encrypted form) that is stolen by hackers at a major risk of being exploited in future.

In addition to posing a threat to current encryption schemes, quantum computing also has the capacity to render blockchain technology highly vulnerable. Since blockchain works on disseminated consensus of trust, which is implemented using public-key cryptography, they are vulnerable to cyberattacks that reveal a user's private key despite being given only the public key (Burns, 2023).

6. AI and ML - The Next Wave

The exponential growth in processing power, along with advancements in voice recognition, facial and image recognition and deep learning autonomous industrial systems, is set to make human-like AI a reality. The promise of greater productivity and cost savings has investments pouring into the development and use of AI and ML in a big way. Meanwhile, threat actors are also getting cleverer, sharpening their techniques and strategies, and using artificial intelligence (AI) and machine learning (ML) to improve the impact of their intrusions and the success rates of their attacks. They are employing AI to develop phishing emails, automate attacks, spread ransomware, rapidly exploit vulnerabilities and even develop complex malware code. For example, they can use ChatGPT to make a phishing email template that can easily be reused.

One of the causalities of the widespread use of AI and ML is the erosion of trust online, which can undermine offline relationships and institutions. It could get increasingly difficult to differentiate between humans and machines. Experts are already ringing alarm bells about deepfake videos (containing hyperrealistic images) and audio messages that are fake or manipulated clips. New images will be created from existing datasets of images, and deepfake videos that can challenge people's perception of realities will proliferate, confusing our ability to discern what is true from false.

There is already a major surge in the use of AI-powered bots to spread disinformation on social media platforms. In the future, AI will not only generate content for launching disinformation campaigns but also disseminate the same through AI-powered bots. It has already become increasingly challenging to distinguish bots from real people, even though historically, machines have failed to pass the Turing Test. The Turing Test, created by mathematician Alan Turing, is a simple method of determining whether a machine can demonstrate human intelligence. The test suggests that if a machine can engage in a conversation with a human being without being detected as a machine, it has demonstrated human intelligence.

A test was conducted by Google using Duplex, an artificial intelligence (AI) technology that simulated a human voice and makes phone calls on a person's behalf. In the test, Duplex succeeded in securing a hairdresser appointment without the human on the other end of the line realising that they were interacting with a machine.

Similarly, in 2014, a computer program called Eugene Goostman, which mimics a teenage Ukrainian boy, is said to have passed the Turing Test at an event organised by the University of Reading (BBC, 2014).

However, critics maintain that these tests do not mean that a machine passed the Turing Test, as the conduct of the tests did not conform to the specific test parameters.

A new version of the Turing Test is conducted by more than one human judge, who interrogate and chat with both subjects. If the interrogator cannot distinguish the computer from the human with greater than 70 per cent accuracy after 5 minutes of interaction with each participant, then the computer is deemed to have passed the test. Experts predict that computers and intelligent bots may, in fact, pass the Turing Test soon, enabling hackers to create bots specialising in spam on platforms like Facebook, Instagram and Twitter that can often outperform humans. This could also be a big inflexion point for the nature and scale of cyberattacks.

According to a recent report, Swift, an artificial intelligence drone pilot, has recently defeated the best human pilots in the world of high-speed drone racing. Developed by researchers at the University of Zurich, the Swift AI won 15 out of 25 races against world champions (humans), and clocked the fastest lap on a course where drones reach speeds of 50mph (80 km/h) and endure accelerations up to 5g, enough to make many people black out. This could be the first time that a robot powered by AI has beaten a human champion in a real physical sport designed for and by humans (Pandey, 2023).

Is this an inflection point?

One of the areas where bots can play a big role is in launching disinformation campaigns. According to the Council of Europe, "propaganda, misinformation and fake news have the potential to polarise public opinion, to promote violent extremism and hate speech and, ultimately, to undermine democracies and reduce trust in the democratic processes" (Council of Europe, n.d).

In August 2023, Meta (parent company of social media platforms like Facebook and Instagram) disrupted a disinformation campaign described by the company as "largest known cross-platform covert influence operation in the world".

In a swift action, Meta took down more than 7,700 accounts and 930 pages on Facebook which were generating and circulating positive posts about China, with a particular focus on positive commentary about the government's treatment of the Uyghur minority group in its Xinjiang province.

According to Meta researchers, the network which was active on other platforms like Medium, Reddit, Tumblr, YouTube and X (formerly known as Twitter), was linked to the Chinese law enforcement (Goswami, 2023).

The use of AI-driven bots as a means to generate and propagate disinformation and fake news is fraught with dangerous consequences. Even today, in addition to the billions of human beings using social media, there are also millions of bots and fake identities which reside within these platforms. There are armies of bots, which are estimated to be between 5-15 per cent of users on social media platforms. Bots can help to propagate fake news by sharing text, images, videos or links online, which enables information to go viral within hours. With new technologies and a greater number of bots, in the future, this can happen in minutes or even seconds. This could be causing great harm to communities and society at large by the rapid spread of fake news, hate speech, and other social issues.

It is increasingly difficult to distinguish bots from real people and, therefore, difficult to control the spread of disinformation. Average social media users are likely to trust what they see or what is shared by others without questioning it. A future of multi-purpose AI bot-driven campaigns is inevitable and would take efforts from all sections of society, like governments, regulators, social media platform owners and the common people, to mitigate and counter them.

Skilled hackers using AI are creating several avenues for stealing and scamming innocent victims by luring them into unwittingly downloading disguised malware. While hackers have been using such mechanisms in the past, the quality and sophistry of AI tools in the future will enable them to create an illusion of authenticity, thereby raising the risks of cyber harm for the victims. Hence, we could see an explosion of scams based on the use of AI. Preventing these types of cybercrimes could be extremely difficult, as human beings are trusting and tend to believe what they see and hear, and act spontaneously and take actions that could even jeopardise their own safety and security.

It is predicted that as early as 2025, the exponential growth of data and information technology could make it possible to form accurate models of every part of the human brain and its 100 billion neurons (Futurebusinesstech, 2022).

In a world of increasingly sophisticated synthetic media and AI-based cyberattacks, cybersecurity solution vendors are incorporating adversarial machine learning algorithms into their solutions to make them evolve and become more robust. However, adversarial machine learning is a technique that is also available to threat actors who can use similar machine learning models to cause cyberattacks. These kinds of attacks, also known as adversarial attacks, are, in effect, capable of turning a machine learning system to work against itself and cause chaos in the organisation running it.

Password cracking is a favourite activity of hackers. It is also the most widely used system for user authentication. For hackers, the password is an important gateway to launch attacks. Traditional authentication systems based on passwords remain a weak point, more so with the advent of AI-based password crackers such as PassGAN. Such AI-based password crackers can guess over half of common passwords in less than a minute. Many organisations and cloud service providers have moved from single-factor authentication to Multi-Factor Authentication (MFA) to add additional layers of protection. Hackers, though, have enhanced their capabilities to enable them to break/bypass MFA and compromise people's accounts. Using AI, passwords can be cracked, and biometrics such as fingerprints and facial images can be faked. Protection from sophisticated phishing attacks requires a toolset that extends beyond MFA and covers multiple attack vectors. More will need to be done from a security point of view using the power of AI, ML and automation to fight fire with fire, along with implementing approaches such as zero-trust.

7. Highly Targeted Cyberattacks

With the easy availability of malware for launching cyberattacks and the growth of Cybercrime-as-a-Service (CaaS) models, hackers can now rent, buy tools for an attack or even pay for them as a share of profits earned. This gives them more time to direct their efforts at researching their targets, who are more likely to pay a ransom or otherwise provide a better return on investment (Filipkowski, 2023).

One of the most potent and disruptive forms of malware is ransomware. Experts say that 2022 was a breakout year for ransomware as it was the hacker's preferred attack vector that inflicted major disruptions and devastation on individuals and organisations around the world. In recent years, ransomware attacks in the form of double extortion and Ransomware-as-a-Service are trends that are likely to continue in the future. As there is a direct and immediate payoff for the groups who are behind ransomware campaigns, they will be highly targeted (to achieve higher success rates) and become a part of larger attacks and concerted campaigns. Given the kind of control that hacker groups can exercise by launching a successful cyberattack, such attacks could be used to meet other objectives, including forcing large corporations and governments to agree to their conditions in return for restoring their data.

From being toys and prototypes, unmanned aerial vehicles (UAVs) or drones are increasingly being deployed for applications such as military surveillance, reconnaissance and combat, disaster relief, agriculture and various commercial applications like parcel delivery, real estate marketing, movie-making, search and rescue missions, medical supply delivery, and more. Multinational giants such as Domino's, UPS and Amazon have started deploying drones to deliver parcels to customers' doorsteps. It is predicted that the worldwide drone market will reach over USD 43 billion by 2024 (Locke, 2021).

The Federal Aviation Administration (FAA) of the USA has projected that the number of commercial unmanned ariel vehicles could reach 835,000 by 2025 (Skygrid, 2023). For threat actors, hacking a drone is akin to hacking a computer. Drone-based cyberattacks can result in outcomes that range from data theft and disruption of services to physical damage or injury. Furthermore, threat actors could hijack weaponised drones to cause physical damage or injury with explosives or other hazardous materials (Skygrid, 2023). Hijacked drones can also be used to redirect drones to a different location by feeding them with false GPS coordinates and even causing them to crash. A hacked drone could potentially serve as a backdoor into an organisation's network and steal sensitive data as well as other confidential information.

Technology is getting increasingly complex over the years, with new innovations being adopted at a frantic pace coexisting with legacy systems. With the number of online users and connected devices increasing everyday, there is a clear divide between those users who are security aware and those devices that are security ready and those who are not. Hence, the opportunity for hackers to find weaknesses and vulnerabilities to launch cyberattacks continues to grow. Cyberattacks in the future will be more sophisticated, potentially more harmful and pose real-world threats. The major threats will come from hacker groups that are organised, have cutting-edge technological skills and have the ability to plan and execute large-scale attacks that could cause widespread damage. Smarter hackers, smarter tools and smarter malware with a large attack surface are a great recipe for the future generation of cyberattacks.

12

Essential Cybersecurity Strategies for the Future

There is no strategy that can provide complete immunity from cyberattacks and cyber shocks. However, cybersecurity strategies and solutions must be deployed to prevent them or minimise the damage.

Cyberattacks and cybercrimes are increasingly threatening the very foundation and sustainability of our modern, digitised society. Our growing dependence on digital infrastructure spreads across public utilities, transportation, shipping, agriculture, telecommunications, healthcare, banking and finance, government, e-commerce, entertainment and emergency services is fraught with various cyber threats and risks. The absence of robust and effective cybersecurity can put individuals, societies, businesses, countries and even the global economy at risk.

Cybersecurity strategies for the future must not only anticipate security challenges that could arise in the future based on new innovations and technological evolution but also include solutions that will address cyber risks that we have not been able to effectively deal with so far.

Prioritise Cybersecurity Literacy

One of the most important areas to improve cybersecurity that demands immediate attention is the lack of basic cybersecurity education and awareness among users. The ability to prevent successful cyberattacks depends on skilled cybersecurity-literate users who can protect themselves and the organisations they may be working for by identifying cyber threats and being able to make the right decisions when confronted with malicious activities that could lead to cyberattacks or becoming victims of ingenious cyber scams. According to the World Economic Forum, 'after reading, writing and arithmetic, the 4th 'r' of literacy is cyber-risk' (World Economic Forum, 2020a). However, for a variety of reasons, it remains the most neglected part of cybersecurity plans and programs.

Various estimates indicate that there are between 2,000 to 4,000 new cyberattacks occurring everyday. Every 14 seconds, a company falls victim to a ransomware attack, which can result in disruptions and financial losses. In addition, 560,000 new pieces of malware are detected everyday. The number one cause of cybersecurity breaches still continues to be the human factor. According to the World Economic Forum, 95 per cent of cybersecurity breaches are caused by human error (World Economic Forum, 2020b).

To address this issue, a multifaceted approach is needed that involves individuals, educational institutions, businesses and government agencies. Such an approach must include the following to improve cybersecurity education and awareness:

- Integrate cybersecurity education into school and university curriculums across disciplines.
- Develop specialised cybersecurity training programs for senior citizens and other sections of society that do not have access to formal education systems. Offer cybersecurity training and workshops to individuals, businesses and government employees.
- Promote and conduct public awareness campaigns on the importance of cybersecurity and its potential risks.
- Develop and distribute free or affordable cybersecurity resources, such as online courses, guides and toolkits. Allocate resources for research and development in cybersecurity technology, which can lead to better tools and solutions for protection against cyber threats.
- Promote large-scale collaboration between government and technology companies to prioritise security in their market offerings.

- Mandate organisations through regulation to meet certain cybersecurity standards, conduct regular cybersecurity training for employees and ensure that they are aware of common threats like phishing and social engineering.
- Share threat intelligence and best practices among stakeholders.
- Encourage and incentivise individuals to enhance cybersecurity skills through advanced and specialised courses and certifications.

Cybersecurity education is not a 'one and done' affair. Continuous evaluation and training are the keys to making every individual ready to battle threats and the shenanigans of threat actors. In the 21st century, cybersecurity must be not only every person's concern but everyone's responsibility, too. The more informed we are, the better equipped we will be to defend ourselves against cyber threats.

Fight AI with AI

According to Bruce Schneier, a public-interest technologist and fellow at the Harvard Kennedy School, "Artificial intelligence will eventually find vulnerabilities in all sorts of social, economic and political systems, and then exploit them at an unprecedented speed, scale and scope. After hacking humanity, AI systems will then hack other AI systems, and humans will be little more than collateral damage". He further goes on to say, "Hackers used to be humans. Soon, AIs will hack humanity" (Schneier, 2021). A very powerful statement of what the future holds.

If threat actors can use AI to gain an offensive advantage, AI can equally be used by defenders to bolster their defences. Cybersecurity solution providers have already started incorporating AI and ML in their solution offerings, which enables them to analyse vast amounts of threat information in real-time and even respond to and prevent cyber threats and attacks. The rising frequency of cyber threats and attacks is forcing organisations (particularly large ones) to use AI-enabled security tools and products that can enable them to detect and respond quickly to cybersecurity incidents with limited or no human intervention.

While traditional antivirus and threat detection software uses AI and ML models to gather, process and use it to form inferences, future security software will also incorporate Deep Learning (DL) models, which can lead to better threat detection and predictions. Deep learning and ML are both advanced forms of AI. DL is a subset of machine learning that uses artificial neural networks to mimic the learning process of the human brain. Deep learning models have the ability to identify complex patterns not only in text but also in pictures, sounds and other data to produce more accurate insights and predictions.

Speed, in both cybersecurity and cyberattacks, will be the key factor that will determine the success of either the attacker or the defender in future. For neutralising cyber threats and preventing cyberattacks in real-time, it is essential that any effective cybersecurity strategy must be based on the use of AI, ML and DL, along with automated response systems.

Apart from threat detection, AI will play an increasingly big role in ensuring better endpoint protection and combating the menace of bots. AI-driven endpoint protection is a way of ensuring that the behaviour of endpoint devices is consistent, observed and controlled. Any deviation from the normal behaviour can be detected and reported for further action. Manual systems are not effective enough to deal with the huge amount of bot traffic that is generated today. AI and ML can help process and classify large volumes of data traffic. AI is a powerful source of innovation in many aspects of our lives. It can offer immense benefits, but it can also cause large-scale harm if misused. In the future, we will witness intense battles between the hackers, who will use AI for malicious purposes, and the defenders, who will employ AI to secure their defences.

Secure Your Information Assets for a Post-Quantum World

A fundamental strategy for the protection of sensitive data and ensuring privacy is the use of encryption. Encryption today is widely used to protect data against cyberattacks and data breaches.

Asymmetric encryption is a popular methodology that encrypts and decrypts the data using two separate cryptographic asymmetric keys—a "public key" and a "private key". Commonly used algorithms for encryption are Triple-DES (3DES), RSA, Diffie-Hellman, Blowfish, Twofish, AES and Elliptic Curve Cryptography. So far, they have proved to be secure and effective.

The advent of quantum computing has the potential to render current encryption methods vulnerable to attack, compromising the security of sensitive data. As we come closer to putting quantum computing to commercial use, organisations must upgrade to quantum-proof or quantum-secure encryption. After all, encryption is the backbone of cybersecurity, which ensures that data and systems are secure.

Quantum-resistant encryption algorithms have the ability to withstand attacks by quantum computers, which could potentially defeat current encryption methods that protect sensitive data. The National Institute of Standards and Technology (NIST), USA, is evaluating various types of quantum-resistant algorithms, such as Lattice-based cryptography, Code-based cryptography, multivariate cryptography, Super singular isogeny-based cryptography, and will soon select the final candidates for the post-quantum cryptographic standard. Organisations must be proactive and implement quantum-resistant algorithms to protect their data from future attacks, as well as HNDL (Harvest Now Decrypt Later) strategies employed by hackers.

Implement Zero-Trust Principles

Digital trust has been declining rapidly in recent years. Threat actors have brazenly and frequently broken through security mechanisms to severely undermine user trust. On the other hand, users, too, are very trusting and are responsible for causing cyberattacks and data breaches.

Digital trust is a complex issue. It requires gaining and maintaining the confidence of all stakeholders and ensuring the safety, privacy, security, reliability and data ethics of their online programs or devices. From a technology perspective, to be trustworthy, technology must be secure (protecting the confidentiality, integrity and availability of connected systems) and must be used responsibly. The lack of guarantees for these basic aspects has inevitably led to a lack of digital trust.

Fixing the crisis of digital trust requires improved technology plus regulatory and industry changes that can help increase trust. At the heart of the problem is the lack of effective authentication mechanisms that can guarantee protection from unauthorised access to systems and data. Threat actors count on gaining unauthorised access and use that to launch cyberattacks and execute large-scale data breaches.

There is still no standard defined as to how systems should stop hackers at the entry point to prevent them from launching repeated assaults and attacks. Organisations use different strategies and methods that they think would help them meet the challenges thrown by threat actors. It is often the case that different stakeholders have different expectations, and therefore, there is no clear assignment of responsibilities between technologies and procedures. A useful strategy for the future is what Huawei, the Chinese technology giant, calls their ABC principle for security. It espouses that a security approach should:

- Assume nothing
- Believe nobody
- Check everything

Fortunately, there are new approaches and concepts like zero-trust, which can help design and deliver products and services that ensure that organisations can adopt a strong stance in promoting digital trust through the deployment of policies, technologies and processes that support the above principles.

Cybersecurity experts are increasingly in agreement that zero-trust has a major role to play in the future of cybersecurity. A zero-trust security solution moves away from the traditional approach of 'trust everyone and everything', to a 'verify, then trust' model. This represents a new way of thinking about cybersecurity. By 2026, the worldwide zero-trust security industry is expected to be worth USD 54.6 billion (Blockchain Council, n.d.). Zero-trust security is based on the premise that no device, user or application should be trusted or given access without verification. It also emphasises the need for defense-in-depth and provides a structure for assessing risk and deciding where to invest in cybersecurity. The zero-trust security model is designed not only to provide protection against external threats but also against insider threats and, therefore, is more effective in preventing data breaches. It further focuses on endpoint protection by limiting access to sensitive data and restricting user privileges. Organisations can implement a zero-trust access model as a core component of future security initiatives, which can also help them in preventing malware, phishing and data exfiltration attacks.

Improve Cyber Incident Response Capabilities

No matter how good your cybersecurity arrangements and mechanisms are, total immunity from cyber threats and attacks is an illusory goal. Hence, organisations must build incident management and response capabilities that can effectively neutralise threats and ward off cyberattacks. The CEO of Forcepoint, the world's biggest cybersecurity company, has predicted that "future cyberattacks could be deadlier than actual wars if rogue elements in the digital underworld take aim at critical infrastructure and connected devices". Gartner, the American technological research and consulting firm, has said that "The dangers of turning technology into a weapon have been flagged in the past, and these can potentially cause harm to humans or kill them by 2025" (Cabral, 2022).

Building response capability to cyber incidents requires a comprehensive set of measures in the form of a playbook, which can be classified into proactive measures and reactive measures.

For large organisations, setting up a next-generation Security Operations Centre (SOC) is a key imperative. The SOC infrastructure must be designed to support business continuity, 24 × 7 perimeter monitoring, early detection and alert generation, AI-based automated vulnerability scanning, threat hunting and constant monitoring of threats and possible attack vectors. Prediction and early detection of complex attacks can help prevent disruption and protect the organisation from the most serious intrusions. Smaller organisations can opt for managed security services operations as they may not be able to make the kind of investments that large organisations can.

Implementation of Security Orchestration, Automation and Response (SOAR), which is a combination of three different technologies—security orchestration and automation, security incident response platforms and threat intelligence platforms—is a 'must have' capability for organisations that are highly vulnerable to frequent cyberattacks. SOAR technologies not only allow organisations to collect and aggregate vast amounts of security data and alerts from multiple sources but also to build automated processes to respond more effectively to low-level security events and standardise threat detection and remediation procedures (Nicholls, 2023).

While these automation initiatives can greatly enhance cybersecurity, the importance of incident response teams in the overall response strategy cannot be undermined. The key goal of the incident response team is to coordinate and align the key resources and team members during a cyber security incident, as well as to minimise impact and restore operations as quickly as possible. It is a vital and essential component of cyber incident response.

Managing Endpoint and Attack Surface

Unmanaged IoT devices can be a source of major cyberattacks. In order to manage any device, it is important for network administrators to have an in-depth visibility of all the devices connected to the network. Endpoint detection and response (EDR) solutions not only provide visibility but also capture all endpoint activity. They also use advanced analytics to provide real-time visibility into the health of all endpoints on a network. In addition, EDR solutions can identify anomalous activity, raise alerts, as well as offer remediation suggestions and capabilities to respond. Furthermore, they can even stop an attack in progress or contain its spread.

When it comes to allowing endpoint devices to be connected to a network, a good practice is to permit only those devices that follow design-in security. A future with more secure IoT devices necessitates building security into the Software Development Life Cycle (SDLC). At a more operational level, it is wise to allow only devices that are supplied by reputed IoT vendors following international standards.

An advancement in EDR is the introduction of Extended Detection and Response (XDR). XDR takes a broader view by integrating security across endpoints, cloud computing, email and other solutions.

Most organisations, large or small, continue to grapple with the problem of an explosion in attack surface. In the future, the attack surface is only going to get bigger and bigger, offering more opportunities for hackers. Zero-trust principles suggest that instead of focusing security efforts on the macro-level of the attack surface, we must identify what we need to protect. A protect surface comprises the data and information assets that need to be protected, the applications that consume sensitive information and the devices and the services that must be protected. Doing this will result in a reduction in attack surface, offering fewer opportunities for threat actors to exploit.

Implement Defense-in-Depth Cybersecurity

Defense-in-depth is a cybersecurity approach that has its origins in military strategy. This is an enduring methodology that involves protecting your IT infrastructure through multiple layers of security protocols rather than relying on any single protective measure. The objective is to lay as many barriers as possible between your valuable data and information and attackers. In the event of failure of one security layer, another one can stop the threat.

Important elements of a defense-in-depth strategy are network security controls, malware protection software, authentication procedures and methods, data encryption, data backups and user awareness training.

A defense-in-depth strategy is a comprehensive and proactive way to protect your system from various types of cyber threats. By implementing multiple layers of security, you can reduce the risk of data breaches and minimise the impact of cyberattacks.

From ubiquitous software-controlled vehicles, Web 3.0, innovations in gaming, virtual reality and hyper-scale Cloud adoption to supply chain frictions, a proliferation of inexpensive tools available to cybercriminals, the emergence of synthetic image generators and fractures in global internet governance, the landscape of digital security is constantly changing—and by 2030, it will once again be radically transformed. Navigating this complex world will require strategic foresight. Those who begin now to look toward this complex new future will have the advantage (Centre for Long Term Cybersecurity, 2023).

There are several security threat scenarios we could face in the future, some of which may go beyond present-day technological capabilities. There are predictions of a doomsday scenario in cyberspace when successive cyberattacks on critical infrastructures around the world could even put a large number of human lives at risk.

Ultimately, the future of cybersecurity is based on effective threat management on a continuous basis. Not only does this require prioritisation, but it also needs the implementation of new concepts and approaches to security management to meet emerging threat scenarios. A greater focus on prevention and preparedness is vital for minimising risk and limiting potential damage.

Cybersecurity is a fast-moving game. If you do not learn to play it well, you may have to pay the price!

References

Abbot, J. (n.d.). *ThreatAware / Discover and Protect Cyber Assets*. Retrieved July 10, 2023, from https://threataware.com/travelex-hacked/

Abrams, L. (2021). *Computer giant Acer hit by $50 million ransomware attack*. https://www.bleepingcomputer.com/news/security/computer-giant-acer-hit-by-50-million-ransomware-attack/

Accesswire. (2022). *6G Cybersecurity Will Transform How We Deal With Cyberattacks*. https://www.accesswire.com/721805/6G-Cybersecurity-Will-Transform-How-We-Deal-With-Cyberattacks

Adams, A. (2019). *Here's What We Know So Far About Russia's 2016 Meddling*. Time. https://time.com/5565991/russia-influence-2016-election/

Agence, F. (2022). *Gang caught running fake Indian cricket league to dupe Russian gamblers / India / The Guardian*. https://www.theguardian.com/world/2022/jul/11/cricket-fake-ipl-tournament-farm-russian-gamblers-india-police-betting-scam-the-sting

Aiello, C. (2018). *Under Armour says data breach affected about 150 million accounts*. https://www.cnbc.com/2018/03/29/under-armour-stock-falls-after-company-admits-data-breach.html

Akash, S. (2023a). *Top 10 Internet Scamming Countries in the World in 2023*. https://www.analyticsinsight.net/top-10-internet-scamming-countries-in-the-world-in-2023/

Akash, S. (2023b). *Top 10 Internet Scamming Countries in the World in 2023*. https://www.analyticsinsight.net/top-10-internet-scamming-countries-in-the-world-in-2023/

Alpspach, K. (2022). *Microsoft Azure vulnerabilities pose new cloud security risk - Protocol*. https://www.protocol.com/enterprise/microsoft-azure-vulnerabilities-cloud-security

Al-Sibai, N. (2022). *Scammer Fools Woman Into Thinking They're an Astronaut Who Needs a Ticket Home*. https://futurism.com/the-byte/iss-scammer-catfish

Anchore. (2022). *2022 Security Trends: Software Supply Chain Survey • Anchore*. https://anchore.com/blog/2022-security-trends-software-supply-chain-survey/

ANI. (2023). *Crypto fraudsters impersonating as Canada officials raided by CBI; Rs 1 cr recovered*. https://www.aninews.in/news/business/business/crypto-fraudsters-impersonating-as-canada-officials-raided-by-cbi-rs-1-cr-recovered20230726175428/

ANI News. (2023). *EP-66 | Trapping ISI agents, cyber espionage & defending India's digital assets with Pavithran Rajan - YouTube*. https://www.youtube.com/watch?v=KS6ONT3i0m4

Applied Materials. (n.d.). *Our Story*. Retrieved July 19, 2023, from https://www.appliedmaterials.com/us/en/about/our-story.html

Arctic Wolf. (2023). *Biggest Retail Industry Cyber Attacks | Arctic Wolf*. https://arcticwolf.com/resources/blog/10-major-retail-industry-cyber-attacks/

Barner, K. (2023). *The Long Tail of a Supply Chain Cyber Attack*. https://www.linkedin.com/pulse/long-tail-supply-chain-cyber-attack-kelly-barner

BBC. (n.d.). *Why so many people fall for scams - BBC Worklife*. Retrieved August 6, 2023, from https://www.bbc.com/worklife/article/20180727-why-so-many-people-fall-for-scams

BBC. (2013a). *Burger King Twitter account "hacked" with McDonald's logo - BBC News*. https://www.bbc.com/news/world-us-canada-21500175

BBC. (2013b). *Cybercriminals "drained ATMs" in $45m world bank heist - BBC News*. https://www.bbc.com/news/world-us-canada-22470299

BBC. (2014). *Computer AI passes Turing test in "world first" - BBC News*. https://www.bbc.com/news/technology-27762088

BBC. (2017). *Ransomware cyber-attack: Who has been hardest hit? - BBC News*. https://www.bbc.com/news/world-39919249

BBC. (2022). *JBS: Cyber-attack hits world's largest meat supplier - BBC News*. https://www.bbc.com/news/world-us-canada-57318965

BBC News. (2013). *Dick Cheney: Heart implant attack was credible - BBC News*. https://www.bbc.com/news/technology-24608435

Beg, O. (2023). *Why 2023 is the year for software supply chain attacks*. https://hadrian.io/blog/why-2023-is-the-year-for-software-supply-chain-attacks

Bhardwaj, P. (2022). *What is the SolarWinds Cyber Attack*. Bhardwaj, Pranav. https://www.tutorialspoint.com/what-is-the-solarwinds-cyber-attack

Bhati, D. (2023a). *Indians losing lakhs to the new courier scam: What is happening, how to stay safe - India Today*. https://www.indiatoday.in/technology/news/story/indians-losing-lakhs-to-the-new-courier-scam-what-is-happening-how-to-stay-safe-2399043-2023-06-28

Bhati, D. (2023b). *Man receives Rs 150 after liking YouTube videos, ends up losing Rs 40 lakh in the online scam - India Today*. https://www.indiatoday.in/technology/news/story/man-receives-rs-150-after-liking-youtube-videos-ends-losing-rs-40-lakh-in-the-online-scam-2406421-2023-07-14

Bisson, D. (2021). *REvil Ransomware Gang Tells All About Alliances, Revenue*. https://securityintelligence.com/news/revil-ransomware-gang-tells-all-alliances-revenue/

Bizga, A. (2023). *Cybercriminals exploit human misery in earthquake-hit Turkey and Syria with new online disaster scam*. https://www.bitdefender.com/blog/hotforsecurity/cybercriminals-exploit-human-misery-in-earthquake-hit-turkey-and-syria-with-new-online-disaster-scam/

Blockchain Council. (n.d.). *The Future of Cybersecurity: How Zero Trust Security is Revolutionizing Business Protection - Blockchain Council*. Retrieved September 4, 2023, from https://www.blockchain-council.org/info/the-future-of-cybersecurity-how-zero-trust-security-is-revolutionizing-business-protection/

Brading, A. (2011). *Xbox Live customers not hacked but phished – Naked Security*. https://nakedsecurity.sophos.com/2011/11/22/xbox-live-customers-not-hacked-but-phished/

Burns, R. (2023). *The cybersecurity implications of quantum computing/ Security Info Watch*. https://www.securityinfowatch.com/cybersecurity/information-security/managed-network-security/article/53012965/the-cybersecurity-implications-of-quantum-computing

Burt, J. (n.d.). *Report: Cloud-based networks under growing attack • The Register*. 2023. Retrieved May 22, 2023, from https://www.theregister.com/2023/01/20/cloud_networks_under_attack/

Business Wire. (2020). *Kaspersky Report: Criminals Targeted Remote Work In 2020 / Business Wire*. https://www.businesswire.com/news/home/20201210005650/en/Kaspersky-Report-Criminals-Targeted-Remote-Work-In-2020

BusinessInsider. (n.d.). *Max Ray "Iceman" Butler / Business Insider India*. Retrieved July 4, 2023, from https://www.businessinsider.in/The-12-most-infamous-hackers-of-all-time/Max-Ray-Iceman-Butler/slideshow/52453972.cms

Cabral, A. (2022). *Future cyber attacks "could be deadlier than wars."* https://www.msn.com/en-ae/news/world/future-cyber-attacks-could-be-deadlier-than-wars/ar-AA12Ew4q

Center for Internet Security. (n.d.). *The Mirai Botnet – Threats and Mitigations*. Retrieved August 20, 2023, from https://www.cisecurity.org/insights/blog/the-mirai-botnet-threats-and-mitigations

Centre for Long Term Cybersecurity. (2023). *Cybersecurity Futures 2030 - CLTC*. https://cltc.berkeley.edu/program/cybersecurity-futures-2030/

CFR. (2012). *Compromise of Saudi Aramco and RasGas / CFR Interactives*. https://www.cfr.org/cyber-operations/compromise-saudi-aramco-and-rasgas

Cimpanu, C. (2019). *French gas stations robbed after forgetting to change gas pump PINs / ZDNET*. https://www.zdnet.com/article/french-gas-stations-robbed-after-forgetting-to-change-gas-pump-pins/

Cimpanu, C. (2022). *SEC filings: SolarWinds says 18,000 customers were impacted by recent hack / ZDNET*. https://www.zdnet.com/article/sec-filings-solarwinds-says-18000-customers-are-impacted-by-recent-hack/

CISA. (n.d.). *Incident Reporting System / CISA*. Retrieved May 7, 2023, from https://www.cisa.gov/forms/report

CISA. (2020). *CISA National Cyber Incident Scoring System (NCISS)/ CISA*. https://www.cisa.gov/news-events/news/cisa-national-cyber-incident-scoring-system-nciss

Ciso-portal.com. (2021). *Reasons Why Cybersecurity Awareness is Important - CISO Portal*. https://www.ciso-portal.com/reasons-why-cybersecurity-awareness-is-important/

Clark, K. (2022). *The Drum / Yahoo Lawsuit Alleges Employee Stole Trade Secrets Upon Receiving Trade Desk Job Offer*. https://www.thedrum.com/news/2022/05/19/yahoo-lawsuit-alleges-employee-stole-trade-secrets-upon-receiving-trade-desk-job

CoinTelegraph. (2023). *17 biggest crypto heists of all time*. https://cointelegraph.com/explained/the-biggest-crypto-heists-of-all-time

Cook, S. (2023). *50+ Ransomware Statistics & Facts for 2018-2022*. https://www.comparitech.com/antivirus/ransomware-statistics/

Cooke, T. (2023). *Microsoft Data Breaches History & Full Timeline Up To 2023 - EarthWeb*. https://earthweb.com/microsoft-data-breaches/

Council of Europe. (n.d.). *Dealing with propaganda, misinformation and fake news - Democratic Schools for All*. Retrieved September 2, 2023, from https://www.coe.int/en/web/campaign-free-to-speak-safe-to-learn/dealing-with-propaganda-misinformation-and-fake-news

Craft, D. (2023). *Malware Statistics & Facts: Frequency, Impact & Cost*. https://www.worthinsurance.com/post/malware-statistics

Crothers, B. (2022). *Conti Ransomware Group Attacks Costa Rica, U.S. Responds With $15 Million Bounty / Venafi*. https://venafi.com/blog/conti-ransomware-group-attacks-costa-rica-us-responds-15-million-bounty/

CSA. (2022). *Cybersecurity Labelling Scheme for Medical Devices*. https://www.csa.gov.sg/News-Events/Press-Releases/2022/cybersecurity-labelling-scheme-for-medical-devices

Cyber Kendra. (2023). *BlueBleed leaks: Microsoft Exposed 2.4 TB of Business Customer Data - Cyber Kendra*. https://www.cyberkendra.com/2022/10/bluebleed-leaks-microsoft-exposed-24-tb.html#gsc.tab=0

Dirchi, R. (2023). *Are Hardware Wallets Secure? 3 Common Crypto Scams To Watch Out*. https://www.outlookindia.com/business/are-hardware-wallets-secure-3-common-crypto-scams-to-watch-out-news-254793

DOJ. (2023). *Office of Public Affairs | Russian Nationals Charged With Hacking One Cryptocurrency Exchange and Illicitly Operating Another / United States Department of Justice*. https://www.justice.gov/opa/pr/russian-nationals-charged-hacking-one-cryptocurrency-exchange-and-illicitly-operating-another

Douthwaite, A. (2022). *Cybercrime's Evolution Since the 80's: Historical Facts.* https://virtualarmour.com/cybercrimes-evolution-since-the-80s/

Dragonetti, D. (n.d.). *What is an Endpoint? Tech, Threats & Security For 2023.* Retrieved May 22, 2023, from https://www.selecthub.com/endpoint-security/what-is-endpoint/

Eaton, C., & Volz, D. (2021). *Colonial Pipeline CEO Tells Why He Paid Hackers a $4.4 Million Ransom - WSJ.* https://www.wsj.com/articles/colonial-pipeline-ceo-tells-why-he-paid-hackers-a-4-4-million-ransom-11621435636

ENISA. (2022). *Incident Reporting — ENISA.* https://www.enisa.europa.eu/topics/incident-reporting

ENISA. (2023). *Identifying Emerging Cyber Security Threats And Challenges For 2030 March 2023 Identifying Emerging Cyber Security Threats And Challenges For 2030 About ENISA.* https://doi.org/10.2824/117542

Ermetic. (2022). *The Cost of a Data Breach in 2022 / CSA.* https://cloudsecurityalliance.org/blog/2022/12/02/ibm-cost-of-a-data-breach-2022-highlights-for-cloud-security-professionals/

Exabeam. (n.d.). *Insider Threat Examples: 3 Famous Cases and 4 Preventive Measures.* Retrieved May 16, 2023, from https://www.exabeam.com/explainers/insider-threat/insider-threat-examples/

FBI. (2021). *FBI Statement on Compromise of Colonial Pipeline Networks — FBI.* https://www.fbi.gov/news/press-releases/fbi-statement-on-compromise-of-colonial-pipeline-networks

Filipkowski, B. (2023). *What is the future of cybersecurity? / Field Effect.* https://fieldeffect.com/blog/what-is-the-future-of-cyber-security

Financial Times. (n.d.). *Maersk CEO Soren Skou on surviving a cyber-attack.*

Fox, J. (2022). *Top Cybersecurity Statistics to Know for 2023 / Cobalt.* https://www.cobalt.io/blog/cybersecurity-statistics-2023

Franceschi-Biccheirai. Lorenzo. (2023). *Hackers could remotely turn off lights, honk, mess with Tesla's infotainment system / TechCrunch.* https://techcrunch.com/2023/03/28/hackers-could-remotely-turn-off-lights-honk-mess-with-teslas-infotainment-system/?guccounter=1

Frankenfield, J. (2022). *Zero-Day Attack Definition*. https://www.investopedia.com/terms/z/zero-day-attack.asp

Franklin Curtis. (2017). *FDA Warns Abbott on IoT Vulnerability & More / Light Reading*. https://www.lightreading.com/iot/fda-warns-abbott-on-iot-vulnerability-and-more/d/d-id/732127

Frost & Sullivan. (2020). *Frost & Sullivan Analyzes the Future of Privacy and Cybersecurity*. https://www.frost.com/news/press-releases/frost-sullivan-analyzes-the-future-of-privacy-and-cybersecurity/

Furtado, C. (2016). *How did Yahoo! fall from $125 billion to $5 billion in 15 years? / Zee Business*. https://www.zeebiz.com/companies/news-how-did-yahoo-fall-from-125-billion-to-5-billion-in-15-years-4200

Futurebusinesstech. (2022). *The World in 2030: Top 20 Future Technologies*. https://www.futurebusinesstech.com/blog/the-world-in-2030-top-20-future-technologies

Gartner. (n.d.). *Definition of Operational Technology (OT) - Gartner Information Technology Glossary*. Retrieved August 20, 2023, from https://www.gartner.com/en/information-technology/glossary/operational-technology-ot

Gatlan, S. (2019). *Scammers Behind €10 Million BEC Fraud Arrested in Spain*. https://www.bleepingcomputer.com/news/security/scammers-behind-10-million-bec-fraud-arrested-in-spain/

Gilmer, M. (2016). *Millions of email names, passwords hacked in giant data breach, report says | Mashable*. https://mashable.com/article/email-data-breach

GlobeNewWire. (2021). *Scammers Are Winning: €41.3 ($47.8) Billion Lost in Scams,*. https://www.globenewswire.com/en/news-release/2021/10/14/2313978/0/en/Scammers-Are-Winning-41-3-47-8-Billion-Lost-in-Scams-Up-15.html

Goswami, R. (2023). *Meta disrupts Chinese misinformation network linked to law enforcement*. https://www.cnbc.com/amp/2023/08/29/meta-disrupts-chinese-misinformation-network-linked-to-law-enforcement-.html

Goud, N. (n.d.). *Cyber Attack on American University network makes IoT search for 'Seafood' - Cybersecurity Insiders*. Retrieved July 3, 2023, from https://www.cybersecurity-insiders.com/cyber-attack-on-american-university-network-makes-iot-search-for-seafood/

Government of Western Australia. (n.d.). *scamnet*. Retrieved August 10, 2023, from https://www.scamnet.wa.gov.au/scamnet/Scam_types-Threats__extortion-Hitman_Scams-Hitman_Scam.htm

Green, A. (2018). *Facebook's 52,000 data points on each person reveal something shocking about its future - Komando.com*. https://www.komando.com/social-media/facebooks-52000-data-points-on-each-person-reveal-something-shocking-about-its-future/489188/

Grey, M. (2020). *REvil – GSMS Data Breach: Grubman Hackers Threaten Trump w/ Data Leak*. https://news.hackreports.com/revil-hacks-gsms-data-breach-donald-trump-lady-gaga-madonna-data-leak-on-dark-web/

Griffiths, C. (2023a). *The Latest Phishing Statistics (updated August 2023) / AAG IT Support*. https://aag-it.com/the-latest-phishing-statistics/

Griffiths, C. (2023b). *The Latest Ransomware Statistics (updated June 2023) / AAG IT Support*. https://aag-it.com/the-latest-ransomware-statistics/

Grigutyte, M. (2023). *The Nigerian Prince scam: Everything you need to know / NordVPN*. https://nordvpn.com/blog/nigerian-prince-scam/

Grosser, S. (2022). *Micitt: "desde ayer no se han registrado nuevos incidentes informáticos" - Delfino.cr*. 2022. https://delfino.cr/2022/04/micitt-desde-ayer-no-se-han-registrado-nuevos-incidentes-informaticos

Hattar, M. (2021). *Great Power or Great Vulnerability? Securing 5G and 6G Networks - SecurityWeek*. https://www.securityweek.com/great-power-or-great-vulnerability-securing-5g-and-6g-networks/

Haworth, J. (2020). *What is Sodinokibi? The ransomware behind the Travelex attack / The Daily Swig*. https://portswigger.net/daily-swig/what-is-sodinokibi-the-ransomware-behind-the-travelex-attack

Heilingenstein, M. (2023). *Facebook Data Breaches: Full Timeline Through 2023*. https://firewalltimes.com/facebook-data-breach-timeline/

Helmke Mathew. (2019). *After the Retrospective: Dyn DDoS*. https://www.gremlin.com/blog/after-the-retrospective-dyn-ddos/

Help Net Security. (2003). *Sobig Virus Damage Breaks World Record - Help Net Security*. https://www.helpnetsecurity.com/2003/08/30/sobig-virus-damage-breaks-world-record/

Henriquez, M. (2022). *Swissport operations impacted by ransomware attack / Security Magazine*. https://www.securitymagazine.com/articles/97038-swissport-operations-impacted-by-ransomware-attack

Hernandez, J. (2021). *The Russian hacker group behind the SolarWinds attack is at it again, Microsoft says : NPR*. https://www.npr.org/2021/10/25/1048982477/russian-hacker-solarwinds-attack-microsoft

Hersher, R. (2015). *Meet Mafiaboy, The "Bratty Kid" Who Took Down The Internet : All Tech Considered : NPR*. https://www.npr.org/sections/alltechconsidered/2015/02/07/384567322/meet-mafiaboy-the-bratty-kid-who-took-down-the-internet

Higgins Jackson Kelly. (2008). *Hacker's Choice: Top Six Database Attacks*. https://www.darkreading.com/risk/hacker-s-choice-top-six-database-attacks

Huawei. (2023). *Computing 2030*.

Huddleston, T. J. (2019). *Phishing email scam stole $100 million from Facebook and Google*. https://www.cnbc.com/2019/03/27/phishing-email-scam-stole-100-million-from-facebook-and-google.html

IANS. (2019). *Aadhaar data breach report incorrect: HC told / Mint*. https://www.livemint.com/news/india/aadhaar-data-breach-report-incorrect-hc-told-1550145892105.html

IBM. (n.d.). *What is Shadow IT? / IBM*. Retrieved May 22, 2023, from https://www.ibm.com/topics/shadow-it

IDC. (2020). *How much data will there be in 2030?* https://osgamers.com/frequently-asked-questions/how-much-data-will-there-be-in-2030

IDC. (2021). *Future of Industry Ecosystems: Shared Insights & Data/ IDC Blog*. https://blogs.idc.com/2021/01/06/future-of-industry-ecosystems-shared-data-and-insights/

IEC. (2023). *Protecting medical devices and hospitals against cyber-attacks / IEC*. https://iec.ch/blog/protecting-medical-devices-and-hospitals-against-cyber-attacks

Ikeda, S. (2023). *Major Semiconductor Firm Applied Materials Hit by Supply Chain Attack; Ransomware Impact Will Cost $250 Million - CPO Magazine*. https://www.cpomagazine.com/cyber-security/major-semiconductor-firm-applied-materials-hit-by-supply-chain-attack-ransomware-impact-will-cost-250-million/

Imperva. (n.d.). *Trojans*. Retrieved May 12, 2023, from https://www.imperva.com/learn/application-security/trojans/

India News. (2023). *New Rules For SIM Verification: Key Points To Know*. https://www.ndtv.com/india-news/new-rules-for-sim-verification-key-points-to-know-4307833#pfrom=home-ndtv_topstories

Innefu Labs. (n.d.). *HOW CYBER SECURITY IMPACTS BUSINESSES GLOBALLY?* Retrieved June 6, 2023, from https://www.innefu.com/blog/how-cyber-security-impacts-businesses-globally/

Irving, M. (2021). *IBM unleashes the Eagle, the world's most powerful quantum processor*. https://newatlas.com/quantum-computing/ibm-eagle-quantum-processor/

ISBUZZ Staff. (2022). *Global Cybersecurity Study: Insider Threats Cost Organizations $15.4 Million Annually, Up 34 Percent From 2020*. https://informationsecuritybuzz.com/global-cybersecurity-study-insider-threats-cost-organizations-15-4-million-annually-up-34-percent-from-2020/

James, N. (2023). *💬1 - 81 Phishing Attack Statistics 2023: The Ultimate Insight*. https://www.getastra.com/blog/security-audit/phishing-attack-statistics/

Johnson, A. (2020). *The Devastating Effect Of Polymorphic Malware*. https://cybersecurityventures.com/the-devastating-effect-of-polymorphic-malware/

Kerner, M. S. (2022). *Log4j explained: Everything you need to know*. https://www.techtarget.com/whatis/feature/Log4j-explained-Everything-you-need-to-know

Kost, E. (2023). *Log4Shell: The Log4j Vulnerability Emergency Clearly Explained | UpGuard*. https://www.upguard.com/blog/apache-log4j-vulnerability

Kovacs, E. (2017). *NotPetya Attack Costs Big Companies Millions - SecurityWeek*. https://www.securityweek.com/notpetya-attack-costs-big-companies-millions/

KuCoin. (n.d.). *About Us / KuCoin*. Retrieved July 28, 2023, from https://www.kucoin.com/about-us

Lakshmanan, R. (2022). *Microsoft Mitigated Record-Breaking 3.47 Tbps DDoS Attack on Azure Customers*. https://thehackernews.com/2022/01/microsoft-mitigated-record-breaking-347.html

Leonhordt, M. (2019). *Nigerian prince scams still rake in over $700,000 a year*. https://www.cnbc.com/2019/04/18/nigerian-prince-scams-still-rake-in-over-700000-dollars-a-year.html

Leyden John. (2020). *XSS vulnerability in 'Login with Facebook' button earns $20,000 bug bounty / The Daily Swig*. https://portswigger.net/daily-swig/xss-vulnerability-in-login-with-facebook-button-earns-20-000-bug-bounty

Liu, N. (2022). *Expeditors International Shuts Down Computer Systems After Cyberattack*. https://www.wsj.com/articles/expeditors-international-shuts-down-computer-systems-after-cyberattack-11645566461?tpl=cs

Locke, J. (2021). *Can Drones Be Hacked, Tracked, and Used to Carry Passengers? / Digi International*. https://www.digi.com/blog/post/can-drones-be-hacked-tracked-and-carry-passengers

Lucas, E. (2019). *The Spycraft Revolution – Foreign Policy*. https://foreignpolicy.com/2019/04/27/the-spycraft-revolution-espionage-technology/

Magnusson, A. (2023). *What is a Brute Force Attack? Types, Examples & Prevention / StrongDM*. https://www.strongdm.com/blog/brute-force-attack

Malwarebyte Labs. (2021). *150,000 Verkada security cameras hacked—to make a point*. https://www.malwarebytes.com/blog/news/2021/03/150000-verkada-security-cameras-hacked-to-make-a-point

Martin, A. (2022). *Mondelez and Zurich reach settlement in NotPetya cyberattack insurance suit*. https://therecord.media/mondelez-and-zurich-reach-settlement-in-notpetya-cyberattack-insurance-suit

Masjedi, Y. (2023). *The Worst Social Media Scams of 2023 (How To Avoid Them)*. https://www.aura.com/learn/social-media-scams#2.-Romance-scams

McArthur, L. (2017). *Dr Christopher Frei, Secretary...: 24 May 2017: Scottish Parliament debates - TheyWorkForYou*. https://www.theyworkforyou.com/sp/?id=2017-05-24.19.14

McCallum, S. (2022). *Meta settles Cambridge Analytica scandal case for $725m - BBC News*. https://www.bbc.com/news/technology-64075067

McCormick, R. (2014). *Hackers made Iran's nuclear computers blast AC/DC - The Verge*. https://www.theverge.com/2014/8/7/5977885/hackers-made-irans-nuclear-computers-blast-ac-dc

Mcfarland, M. (2021). *Don't fill plastic bags with gas, safety agency warns / CNN Business*. https://edition.cnn.com/2021/05/12/cars/gas-plastic-bags-safety/index.html

Mclean, M. (2023). *2023 Must-Know Cyber Attack Statistics and Trends / Embroker*. https://www.embroker.com/blog/cyber-attack-statistics/

McMillan, R. (2014). *The Inside Story of Mt. Gox, Bitcoin's $460 Million Disaster / WIRED*. https://www.wired.com/2014/03/bitcoin-exchange/

Meige, A. (2023). *Five Expert Predictions for the Future of Quantum Computing*. https://www.quantumbusinessnews.com/research/five-expert-predictions-for-the-future-of-quantum-computing-

Menon, V. (2022). *Kolkata is India's newest, biggest scam zone. Police, YouTubers, mice can't shut it down*. https://theprint.in/feature/kolkata-is-indias-newest-biggest-scam-zone-police-youtubers-mice-cant-shut-it-down/1035160/

Microsoft. (2023). *State of cybercrime / Microsoft Security*. https://www.microsoft.com/en-in/security/business/microsoft-digital-defense-report-2022-state-of-cybercrime

Millis, E. (2010). *New IE hole exploited in attacks on U.S. firms - CNET*. https://www.cnet.com/news/privacy/new-ie-hole-exploited-in-attacks-on-u-s-firms/

Model Thinkers. (n.d.). *ModelThinkers - Stability Zones*. Retrieved August 25, 2023, from https://modelthinkers.com/mental-model/stability-zones

Money Control. (2023). *Economic Survey 2023: 135.2 crore Aadhaar numbers generated till November 2022*. https://www.moneycontrol.com/news/business/budget/economic-survey-2023-135-2-crore-aadhaar-numbers-generated-till-november-2022-9971821.html

Mora Por Andrea. (2022). *Chaves afirma que país está en guerra por ataques cibernéticos y que habría ticos ayudando a Conti*

- *Delfino.cr*. https://delfino.cr/2022/05/chaves-afirma-que-pais-esta-en-guerra-por-ataques-ciberneticos-y-que-habria-ticos-ayudando-a-conti

Morgan, S. (2020). *Cybercrime To Cost The World $10.5 Trillion Annually By 2025*. https://cybersecurityventures.com/hackerpocalypse-cybercrime-report-2016/

Morgan, S. (2022). *Cybercrime To Cost The World 8 Trillion Annually In 2023*. https://cybersecurityventures.com/cybercrime-to-cost-the-world-8-trillion-annually-in-2023/

Naidu, J. (2020). *Fake News Detection using Traditional ML and Modern DL Algorithms*. Medium. https://jaswanth20061.medium.com/fake-news-detection-using-traditional-ml-and-modern-dl-methods-669a0907dad

NCSC. (n.d.). *Mitigating malware and ransomware attacks - NCSC.GOV.UK*. Retrieved May 2, 2023, from https://www.ncsc.gov.uk/guidance/mitigating-malware-and-ransomware-attacks

NDTV. (2019). *European Aerospace Airbus Hit By Series Of Cyber Attacks On Suppliers: Report*. https://www.ndtv.com/world-news/european-aerospace-airbus-hit-by-series-of-cyber-attacks-on-suppliers-report-2107471

Netzer, T. (2022). *Why Attack Surface Assessment Tools Are Vital According to Gartner - Ionix*. https://www.ionix.io/blog/attack-surface-assessment-tools-are-needed-says-gartner/

Nicholas, S. (2021). *Accenture sheds more light on August data breach / TechTarget*. https://www.techtarget.com/searchsecurity/news/252508243/Accenture-sheds-more-light-on-August-data-breach

Nicholls, M. (2023). *What is SOAR? (Security Orchestration, Automation and Response) / Redscan*. https://www.redscan.com/news/what-is-security-orchestration-automation-and-response-soar-and-how-does-it-improve-threat-detection-and-remediation/

Nicholson, P. (2022). *Five Most Famous DDoS Attacks and Then Some / A10 Networks*. https://www.a10networks.com/blog/5-most-famous-ddos-attacks/

Niketan, E. (2022). *20(3)/2022-CERT-In Government of India Ministry of Electronics and Information Technology (MeitY)*. www.cert-in.org.in

NIST. (n.d.). *Best Practices in Cyber Supply Chain Risk Management Conference Materials Cyber Supply Chain Best Practices.*

Oladimeji, S., & Kerner, S. M. (2022). *SolarWinds hack explained: Everything you need to know.* https://www.techtarget.com/whatis/feature/SolarWinds-hack-explained-Everything-you-need-to-know

O'Neill, J. (2021). *Virginia woman sentenced for "staggering" $32M coupon scam.* https://nypost.com/2021/10/26/virginia-woman-sentenced-for-staggering-32m-coupon-scam/

O'Neill, J. (2023). *Cyber Crime Lawyer Duped By Fake Car Insurance Offer In Delhi: Cops.* https://www.ndtv.com/delhi-news/cyber-crime-lawyer-duped-by-fake-car-insurance-offer-in-delhi-cops-3998710

Orcutt, M. (2020). *How the North Korean hackers behind WannaCry got away with a stunning crypto-heist | MIT Technology Review.* https://www.technologyreview.com/2020/01/24/276082/lazarus-group-dragonex-chainalysis/

Osborne, C. (2023). *SolarWinds hackers, Nobelium, once again strike global IT supply chains, Microsoft warns / ZDNET.* https://www.zdnet.com/article/solarwinds-hacking-group-nobelium-is-now-targeting-the-global-it-supply-chain-microsoft-warns/

Pal. Anagh. (2023). *Callers beware! Over 31,000 fake customer care numbers are out there to scam you / Business Insider India.* https://www.businessinsider.in/tech/news/callers-beware-over-31000-fake-customer-care-numbers-are-out-there-to-scam-you/articleshow/98207371.cms

Paliery, J. (2015). *The inside story of the biggest hack in history.* https://money.cnn.com/2015/08/05/technology/aramco-hack/index.html

Palmer, D. (2021). *Big jump in RDP attacks as hackers target staff working from home / ZDNET.* https://www.zdnet.com/article/big-jump-in-rdp-attacks-as-hackers-target-staff-working-from-home/

Panda Media Centre. (2022). *What Is DNS Spoofing and How Can You Prevent It? - Panda Security Mediacenter.* https://www.pandasecurity.com/en/mediacenter/security/dns-spoofing/

Pandey, N. (2023). *AI-Powered Drone Beats World-Champion Human Pilots For The First Time.* https://www.ndtv.com/offbeat/

ai-powered-drone-beats-world-champion-human-pilots-for-the-first-time-4350517

Parker, C. (n.d.). *The 5 Scariest Data Breaches in Government - Executech*. Retrieved June 30, 2023, from https://www.executech.com/insights/the-5-scariest-data-breaches-in-government/

Pauli, D. (2015). *Adobe pays US$1.2M plus settlements to end 2013 breach class action • The Register*. https://www.theregister.com/2015/08/17/adobe_settles_claims_for_data_breach/

Petrosyan, K. (2021). *Colonial pipeline outage in the United States underscores risks to energy supplies – Analysis - IEA*. https://www.iea.org/commentaries/colonial-pipeline-outage-in-the-united-states-underscores-risks-to-energy-supplies

Platsis, G. (2023). *What is the Future of Cyberattacks?* https://securityintelligence.com/articles/what-is-the-future-of-cyberattacks/

Plumb, T. (2023). *Road to supply-chain attacks paved with ignorance, human error and shadow IT - SDxCentral*. https://www.sdxcentral.com/articles/analysis/road-to-supply-chain-attacks-paved-with-ignorance-human-error-and-shadow-it/2023/04/

Powell, O. (2022). *Over 77,000 Uber employee details leaked online*. https://www.cshub.com/attacks/news/iotw-over-77000-uber-employee-details-leaked-in-data-breach

Pownall, C. (n.d.). *Maersk NotPetya cyberattack response timeline - Charlie Pownall* ·保. Retrieved May 2, 2023, from https://charliepownall.com/maersk-notpetya-cyberattack-timeline/

Press Trust of India. (n.d.). *CBI Arrests Delhi Crypto Scammer Who Posed As Canadian Government Official*. Retrieved August 7, 2023, from https://www.ndtv.com/india-news/cbi-arrests-delhi-crypto-scammer-who-posed-as-canadian-government-official-4245648

Proofpoint. (n.d.). *What Is Pharming? - Definition, Examples & More| Proofpoint US*. Retrieved August 11, 2023, from https://www.proofpoint.com/us/threat-reference/pharming

PTI. (2023a). *CBI Arrests Delhi Crypto Scammer Who Posed As Canadian Government Official*. https://www.ndtv.com/india-news/cbi-arrests-delhi-crypto-scammer-who-posed-as-canadian-government-official-4245648

PTI. (2023b). *Press Trust of India: Fraudster represents top insurance portal, sells fake car insurance policy to cyber crime lawyer*.

https://www.ptinews.com/news/national/fraudster-represents-top-insurance-portal-sells-fake-car-insurance-policy-to-cyber-crime-lawyer/562411.html

Pundir, P. (n.d.). *The Weird Story Behind Nidhi Razdan's Fake Harvard Job*. 2021. Retrieved July 3, 2023, from https://www.vice.com/en/article/n7vq8m/india-nidhi-razdan-phishing-scam-harvard-job-offer-fake-cybersecurity

Rabach Jill. (2022). *Alarming attacks on Internet of Medical Things (IoMT).* https://cybersecurity.att.com/blogs/security-essentials/alarming-attacks-on-internet-of-medical-things-iomt

Ray, S. (2018). *BritishAirwaysHack: All it took was 22 lines of code.* https://www.newsbytesapp.com/news/science/22-lines-of-code-got-british-airways-hacked/story

Read, S. (2018). *British Airways boss apologises for "malicious" data breach - BBC News.* https://www.bbc.com/news/uk-england-london-45440850

Reiff. (2023). *The Collapse of FTX: What Went Wrong with the Crypto Exchange?* https://www.investopedia.com/what-went-wrong-with-ftx-6828447

Rocket IT. (2021). *Zoom Vulnerability / Security Risk / Zero Day Breach Update.* https://rocketit.com/zoom-vulnerability-zero-day-security-update/

RUBENSTEIN, M. (2011). *Congratulations, you've won! The reality behind online lotteries / Securelist.* https://securelist.com/congratulations-youve-won-the-reality-behind-online-lotteries/36450/

Savvy Security. (2021). *What Is Email Spoofing? An Explanation.* https://cheapsslsecurity.com/blog/what-is-email-spoofing-an-explanation/

Scarfone, K. A., Grance, T., & Masone, K. (2008). *Computer Security Incident Handling Guide.* https://www.nist.gov/publications/computer-security-incident-handling-guide-0

Schneier, B. (2021). *Hackers Used to Be Humans. Soon, AIs Will Hack Humanity / Belfer Center for Science and International Affairs.* https://www.belfercenter.org/publication/hackers-used-be-humans-soon-ais-will-hack-humanity

Schram, J. (2016). *Congresswoman wants probe of 'brazen' $81M theft from New York Fed.* https://nypost.com/2016/03/22/

congresswoman-wants-probe-of-brazen-81m-theft-from-new-york-fed/

Security Scorecard. (2021). *5 Common Cybersecurity Vulnerabilities in the IoMT.* https://securityscorecard.com/blog/common-cybersecurity-vulnerabilities-in-the-iomt/

Segun, D. (2019). *Sweet Revenge! Tobias Fromel Hacks His Hackers - SecureBlitz.* https://secureblitz.com/tobias-fromel-hacks-his-hackers/

Selyukh, A. (2017). *Yahoo Hack Likely Breached 3 Billion Accounts, All That Existed In Mid-2013 : The Two-Way : NPR.* https://www.npr.org/sections/thetwo-way/2017/10/03/555016024/every-yahoo-account-that-existed-in-mid-2013-was-likely-hacked

Sharma, A. (2022). *BlackCat (ALPHV) claims Swissport ransomware attack, leaks data.* https://www.bleepingcomputer.com/news/security/blackcat-alphv-claims-swissport-ransomware-attack-leaks-data/

Sienko, C. (2016). *The Breach of Anthem Health - the Largest Healthcare Breach in History / Infosec Resources.* https://resources.infosecinstitute.com/topic/the-breach-of-anthem-health-the-largest-healthcare-breach-in-history/

Sigalos, M. (2023). *Sam Bankman-Fried sentence: Could be 100-plus years, or mere decades.* https://www.cnbc.com/2023/11/04/sam-bankman-fried-sentence-could-be-100-plus-years-or-mere-decades.html

Simpson, A. (2022). *11 Real-Life Insider Threat Examples - Code42.* https://www.code42.com/blog/insider-threat-examples-in-real-life/

Singh, K. P. (2023). *The SIM collector of Murshidabad who helps cyber scammers / Latest News India - Hindustan Times.* https://www.hindustantimes.com/india-news/dubaibased-businessman-loses-10-lakh-in-indian-bank-scam-investigation-leads-to-underground-cyber-fraud-machinery-101690223473889.html

Singhal, N. (2017). *Aftermath of WannaCry - BusinessToday - Issue Date: Sep 10, 2017.* https://www.businesstoday.in/magazine/technology/story/wannacry-ransomwarecomputershackersattackransomwarebitcoinscryptocurrencyvirtual-currencymonero-83753-2017-08-21

Skope. (2015). *BEWARE: STUDENT LOAN FORGIVENESS SCAMS - Skope Entertainment Inc.* https://skopemag.com/2015/04/07/beware-student-loan-forgiveness-scams

Skygrid. (2023). *Cybersecurity Threats Within UAV Systems - SkyGrid.* https://www.skygrid.com/cybersecurity-threats-within-uav-systems/

Smith. (2017). *Dallas blames hacker for setting off all 156 emergency warning sirens / CSO Online.* https://www.csoonline.com/article/561055/dallas-blames-hacker-for-setting-off-all-156-emergency-warning-sirens.html

Spyscape. (2023). *Dangerous Liaisons: Honey Trap Spies.* https://spyscape.com/article/dangerous-liaisons-honey-trap-spies

Starikova, A. (n.d.). *Top-5 cryptocurrency heists in history (so far) / Kaspersky official blog.* Retrieved July 28, 2023, from https://www.kaspersky.co.in/blog/top-5-cryptocurrency-heists/24794/

Statista. (2016). *IoT devices installed base worldwide 2015-2025 / Statista.* https://www.statista.com/statistics/471264/iot-number-of-connected-devices-worldwide/

Stempel, J. (2019). *Yahoo strikes $117.5 million data breach settlement after earlier accord rejected / Reuters.* https://www.reuters.com/article/us-verizon-yahoo-idUSKCN1RL1H1

Stupp, C. (2019). *Fraudsters Used AI to Mimic CEO's Voice in Unusual Cybercrime Case - WSJ.* https://www.wsj.com/articles/fraudsters-use-ai-to-mimic-ceos-voice-in-unusual-cybercrime-case-11567157402

Sudhir, U. (2023). *"Even A Techie Lost Rs 82 Lakh": Cops Bust Rs 700-Crore Cyber Fraud Ring.* https://www.ndtv.com/india-news/15-000-indians-conned-of-rs-700-crore-fraudsters-have-china-terror-links-4236308

Thathoo, C. (2022). *Hackers Demand INR 200 Cr Crypto Ransom From AIIMS, Delhi Police Refutes Claims.* https://inc42.com/buzz/aiims-delhi-servers-down-for-sixth-day-hackers-demand-inr-200-cr-in-crypto/

The Week. (2017). *Facebook admits it has 270 million fake accounts.* https://www.theweek.in/news/sci-tech/facebook-admits-it-has-270-million-fake-accounts.html

The White House. (2021). *Executive Order on Improving the Nation's Cybersecurity / The White House.* https://www.whitehouse.gov/

briefing-room/presidential-actions/2021/05/12/executive-order-on-improving-the-nations-cybersecurity/

Tidy, J. (2020). *Major US Twitter accounts hacked in Bitcoin scam - BBC News*. https://www.bbc.com/news/technology-53425822

Toulas, B. (2022). *Swissport ransomware attack delays flights, disrupts operations*. https://www.bleepingcomputer.com/news/security/swissport-ransomware-attack-delays-flights-disrupts-operations/

Tsuchiya, Y., & Hiramoto, N. (2021). How cryptocurrency is laundered: Case study of Coincheck hacking incident. *Forensic Science International: Reports*, *4*. https://doi.org/10.1016/j.fsir.2021.100241

Umawing, J. (2019). *Threat Spotlight: Sodinokibi ransomware attempts to fill GandCrab void / Malwarebytes Labs*. https://www.malwarebytes.com/blog/news/2019/07/threat-spotlight-sodinokibi-ransomware-attempts-to-fill-gandcrab-void

US-CERT. (n.d.). *US-CERT Federal Incident Notification Guidelines Notification Requirement*. Retrieved May 7, 2023, from https://www.dni.gov/cyber-threat-framework/lexicon.html

Vailshery, L. S. (2023). *IoT connected devices worldwide 2019-2030 | Statista*. https://www.statista.com/statistics/1183457/iot-connected-devices-worldwide/

Verge. (2017). *The Ashley Madison hack: everything you need to know - The Verge*. https://www.theverge.com/2015/8/19/9178965/ashley-madison-hacked-news-data-names-list

Vigderman, A., & Gabe, T. (2023). *Does Antivirus Stop Hackers or Provide Hacking Protection?* https://www.security.org/antivirus/hackers/

Vijayan, J. (2013). *Update: Spamhaus hit by biggest-ever DDoS attacks / Computerworld*. https://www.computerworld.com/article/2495967/update--spamhaus-hit-by-biggest-ever-ddos-attacks.html

Vijayan, J. (2022). *Big Questions Remain Around Massive Shanghai Police Data Breach*. https://www.darkreading.com/cloud/questions-massive-shanghai-police-data-breach

Votiro. (2021). *The Facts to Know About the Colonial Pipeline Ransomware Attack / Votiro*. https://votiro.com/blog/the-colonial-pipeline-ransomware-attack-everything-we-know/

Whittaker, Z. (2018). *Marriott says 500 million Starwood guest records stolen in massive data breach / TechCrunch*. https://techcrunch.com/2018/11/30/starwood-hotels-says-500-million-guest-records-stolen-in-massive-data-breach/

Whittaker, Z. (2019). *Some sage security advice after Radiohead's unreleased music hack / TechCrunch*. https://techcrunch.com/2019/06/11/radiohead-hack/

Wilson, T. (2011). *"Night Dragon" Attacks Threaten Major Energy Firms*. https://www.darkreading.com/attacks-breaches/-night-dragon-attacks-threaten-major-energy-firms

Wolfe, N. (2016). *DDoS attack that disrupted internet was largest of its kind in history, experts say / Hacking / The Guardian*. https://www.theguardian.com/technology/2016/oct/26/ddos-attack-dyn-mirai-botnet

Woolf, N. (2015). *DDoS attack that disrupted internet was largest of its kind in history, experts say / Hacking / The Guardian*. https://www.theguardian.com/technology/2016/oct/26/ddos-attack-dyn-mirai-botnet

World Economic Forum. (2020a). *After reading, writing and arithmetic, the 4th "r" of literacy is cyber-risk / World Economic Forum*. https://www.weforum.org/agenda/2020/12/cyber-risk-cyber-security-education/

World Economic Forum. (2020b). *After reading, writing and arithmetic, the 4th "r" of literacy is cyber-risk / World Economic Forum*. https://www.weforum.org/agenda/2020/12/cyber-risk-cyber-security-education/

World Economic Forum. (2023a). *Global Cybersecurity Outlook 2023*.

World Economic Forum. (2023b). *Global Cybersecurity Outlook 2023 J A N U A R Y 2 0 2 3 In collaboration with Accenture Contents*.

Yevura, V. (2022). *Autonomous Vehicles And Their Impact On The Economy*. https://www.forbes.com/sites/forbestechcouncil/2022/02/14/autonomous-vehicles-and-their-impact-on-the-economy/?sh=30916bba60de

Zaheer, A. (2023). *15 Biggest Quantum Computing Companies in the World*. https://finance.yahoo.com/news/15-biggest-quantum-computing-companies-130134308.html